C000301763

BONFIRES ON THE ICE

The Bonfires, by Rudyard Kipling
We know the Rocket's upward whizz;
We know the Boom before the Bust.
We know the whistling Wail which is
The Stick returning to the Dust.
We know how much to take on trust
Of any promised Paradise.
We know the Pie – likewise the Crust.
We know the Bonfire on the Ice.

We know the Mountain and the Mouse.
We know Great Cry and Little Wool.
We know the purseless Ears of Sows.
We know the Frog that aped the Bull.
We know, whatever Trick we pull,
(Ourselves have gambled once or twice)
A Bobtailed Flush is not a Full.
We know the Bonfire on the Ice.

We know that Ones and Ones make Twos –
Till Demos votes them Three or Nought.
We know the Fenris Wolf is loose.
We know what Fight has not been fought.
We know the Father to the Thought
Which argues Babe and Cockatrice
Would play together, were they taught.
We know *that* Bonfire on the Ice.

We know that Thriving comes by Thrift.
We know the Key must keep the Door.
We know his Boot-straps cannot lift
The frightened Waster off the Floor.
We know these things, and we deplore
That not by any Artifice
Can they be altered. Furthermore
We know the Bonfires on the Ice!

BONFIRES ON THE ICE:

THE MULTICULTURAL HARRYING OF BRITAIN

JON GOWER DAVIES

British Library Cataloguing in Publication Data
A catalogue record of this book is available from the British Library

Printed and bound in the United Kingdom

ISBN-13: 978-1-904863-21-2

Social Affairs Unit
314–322 Regent Street
London W1B 5SA
www.socialaffairsunit.org.uk

For Jean. And for my Family and Friends,
near and far, alive and dead.

CONTENTS

ACKNOWLEDGEMENTS

I am grateful to Michael Mosbacher for suggesting that I write this book; and to the Social Affairs Unit both for publishing it and, for some years now, for providing (together with the Liberty Fund) a cheerful and challenging atmosphere and convivial intellectual company. Clive Liddiard copy-read and corrected the text, much improving it. I owe a great deal (including the suggestion for the title) to Norman Dennis, always two steps ahead of the crowd; to John Taylor and Eric Rosby, who read, without too much muttering, the earliest and least coherent versions of my writings; and to my sons Daniel and Jacob, to Ben Hurley, Chris Miller, Hugh Keegan, Paul Fallon, Alan Grint, Steve Ackroyd and Dave Place, who read all or bits of it. Not only did my wife Jean read various drafts, but she also had to tolerate me while I wrote it – not easy.

FOREWORD

As a child of about 10 or 11, I was taken to the National Portrait Gallery. I immediately formed the childish ambition to do something so worthy of note that my picture, too, would one day be found there.

It was childish, no doubt, but not dishonourable; for there is no better way of uniting egotistic ambition and socially beneficial activity than by instilling in someone the desire to preserve and develop a great tradition. And I challenge anyone to assert that there is nothing to be proud of, nothing worthy of emulation, in the long succession of remarkable men and women portrayed in the National Portrait Gallery.

It never occurred to me then or since that, because my mother was a refugee and my paternal grandparents were also refugees, I was somehow debarred from fulfilling my ambition. If I did not fulfil it, the reason was with me alone: lack of talent, lack of application.

As Mr Davis makes clear in his book, this attitude would not at all please or suit the purposes of multiculturalists. Their efforts have been directed not at trying to ensure that every immigrant group integrates into British society, each no doubt bringing something to the feast, but to perpetuating the barriers between groups, and creating a permanent sense of disaffection and unfulfilled entitlement. In so doing, they have created bureaucratic opportunities for themselves and the generally self-selected leaders and spokesmen of immigrant groups, who have profited immensely at the expense of the public purse. They have made a career of nurturing, fostering and perpetuating resentment.

Needless to say, the last thing these political entrepreneurs want is solutions to problems, least of all if they occur spontaneously, without their expensive official ministrations. Their vision of Britain is of a society whose members have very little in common and that is balkanised into a variety of mutually-exclusive mental and sometimes physical ghettoes. In this strange and unworkable vision, which may yet lead to a very unpleasant reaction, the numerically and culturally predominant group is held to be uniquely guilty, *ex officio* as it were, of racism and prejudice. They inherit guilt; minorities inherit innocence.

Mr Davis mocks the pieties of the multiculturalists with some ferocity. It is obvious that some groups are easier to integrate than others, because of the cultural attitudes and attributes they bring with them. This is something that British officialdom refuses to recognise, as if a truth will cease to be a truth if it is ignored for long enough.

The more diverse British society becomes (and even if all immigration were now to cease, the diversity of the geographical origins of its population is an irreversible fact), the more necessary a unifying sense of a national culture becomes. That culture can only be the culture that is recorded in the National Portrait Gallery.

This kind of monoculturalism is, in fact, vastly more generous and accepting of foreigners than a mean-spirited and unimaginative multiculturalism could ever be, with its insistence that people stay in the culture in which they were born, no matter how ill-suited it might be to modern life in these islands. It is not entirely a coincidence that many of the best English prose writers of the twentieth century were not born here: Joseph Conrad, Arthur Koestler, Ernst Gombrich, Karl Popper, Elie Kedourie, to name but a few. These people, who made such a huge contribution to British life, neither received nor expected any special privileges. For them to be accepted was privilege enough.

As Mr Davis points out, all normal procedures have been reversed, so that it is for the host country to understand immigrants, rather than for immigrants to understand the host country. But there is something profoundly dishonest in all this: what precisely (to take a very concrete example) are we supposed to learn from Somalis who make their home here? Their methods of settling political questions, perhaps? Or is it how to chew *khat*? However noble or suited to desert life Somali culture might be, it is clearly not suitable for transfer to Leicester or Middlesbrough. I doubt if more than one in a hundred believers in multiculturalism could specify anything whatever about Somali culture. The Director of Diversity (*sic*) in the last hospital in which I worked thought the Congolese were Muslims and spoke Arabic.

This demonstrates that the real purpose of multiculturalism is job creation for those who either cannot or do not want to work in a genuinely productive field of endeavour. It affords them simultaneously the satisfactions of denouncing their fellow citizens and drawing a salary.

Not everyone will agree with every last assertion made by Mr Davis, but he deserves our gratitude for so fearlessly exposing the absurdity of one of the silliest, but most destructive and dangerous, orthodoxies of our time.

Theodore Dalrymple

INTRODUCTION

While this book is primarily about multiculturalists, a group of intellectuals, policy makers and political activists who 'define the terms' under which various ethno-religious minorities are (or have to be) 'seen', it will inevitably spill over into comment upon such minorities directly. This is in no way, though, to be taken as yet another empirical study of any particular minority or of any groups of them. Furthermore, in discussing multiculturalists, I make little attempt to separate my analysis from my commentary: the two run together, as I am presenting (as will be obvious) an argument, and not simply reporting one. So in Chapter 1, for example, while I describe some of the general characteristics of 'multiculturalists', and some of their main intellectual positions, I also subject one or two of them (both 'ists' and 'isms') to considerable criticism – because I think either that they are wrong or that they exaggerate! Indeed, that is my main criticism throughout: multiculturalists will paint a bit of the story, and then frame it as if it were the entire canvas; they are, almost to a man, polemicists – and quite good ones, too.

In Chapters 2, 3, 4 and 5, I discuss the main features of what, to my mind, is the extraordinarily hostile view that multiculturalists seem to take of the country in which they (or their forebears) have (voluntarily) chosen to live: why, I ask, are they so hostile to the United Kingdom and its history, feel so impelled to tell us how awful we are, and yet queue up to live here? From what culture that is so superior do they come that they feel, for example, quite free to urge the uprooting of our religious institutions or the 're-education' of our public services? Chapter 5 deals with the multicultural attempt to 'reform' our religious institutions. Chapters 7 and 8 have a look at some of the cultures usually left out of the multicultural moral universe. Chapter 6 notes how often multicultural 'spokesmen' or 'spokeswomen' will expostulate at great length and volume about, say, how much worse off financially Pakistani people are than the general population, or how much more likely black men are than white men to be in prison. Apart from the purely technical incompetence of such statements – for an incoming group or their immediate descendants to be on all fours with the natives would be a bizarre statistical miracle – the proper comparator for the financial or social situation of, say, Pakistani women in Britain is the position of Pakistani women *in Pakistan*. If Pakistani women migrate to a Britain in which they are worse off than they would have been had they stayed, or in which they are worse off than those who did stay, then I will eat my statistical hat – and worry about the state of mind of women migrating from the better to the worse. India, discussed in Chapter 7, is the world's biggest democracy and is, in many ways, a multicultural miracle: it has many lessons for us all – not all of them positive or exemplary. Chapter 8 'deals with' Islam. There is no doubt that the entire tone of contemporary multiculturalism takes on a different tone when you mention 'Islam'. Muslims may or may not be proud of this fact – that, for example, in commenting on Islam I feel that I am entering a danger zone, in which an anticipation of a violent response to criticism is far from being evidence of paranoia. I was, in fact, tempted to omit Chapter 8, partly for that reason and partly because Islam is mentioned, inevitably, throughout this book – how could it not be? In spite of this, I have, in Chapter 8, made some fairly terse comments on Islam and Muslims.

Lastly, I have to comment on the extent to which the interests of multiculturalists, and the minorities they claim to represent, dominate our lives. In one week, in what was admittedly a flawed exercise, I calculated that 30–40 per cent of the media coverage of British society came from multiculturalists talking about the minorities who live here. Their demands on us seem huge and incessant: never, I thought, has so much been demanded of so many by so few. It is hard to believe that these 'spokesmen' and 'spokeswomen' are representative of the 2–3 per cent of the population for whom innumerable 'councils' and 'centres' and 'commissions' claim to speak. I do not know how representative they are; but I do know that the net effect of thirty or forty years of multiculturalism has been the creation of what, in India, would be called a 'creamy layer' of vocal and privileged multiculturalists, well ensconced in the 'commanding heights' of British society, well paid, well placed to have and use influence – well placed, that is, to continue to present their small and sectional ambitions and interests as if they were the largest concerns and most urgent business of our troubled society. If this short book can puncture some of that utter pretension, then I will be proud of myself!

CHAPTER 1

STRANGERS WITHIN THE GATE

Two hundred years ago three quarters of the world
lived in some kind of bondage. Freedom, not
slavery, was the peculiar institution.
(Hochschild, 2005: Introduction)

This is not a book about the ethnic minorities who have
arrived here since the end of the Second World War. There are
plenty of good empirical studies about them. It is about
multiculturalists and multiculturalism, a political-intellectual
'Establishment' or 'project' that has both a clear 'mission' and
a related interpretation of history – a 'grand narrative'.

THE MULTICULTURAL 'MISSION STATEMENT'

Briefly, the multicultural 'Mission Statement' insists that the
arrival in Britain since the end of the war of a large variety of
religious and ethnic minorities is problematic only in that, and
when, and for as long as, they, the recently arrived (post-war)
ethno-religious minorities, do not have, or are not given, or
cannot expect to be given, or are in any way frustrated from
inheriting or taking, their due and proper share of the material and cultural capital of British society.

This Mission Statement or ideology can perhaps best be
understood as a kind of Demand Note, or, more gently perhaps, as a *post facto* citizenship application form filled out by
the multiculturalists on behalf (allegedly) of various 'ethnic
minorities' who wish to reside (permanently) in the United
Kingdom, and to become British. The multicultural authors of
such documents are adamant in attesting to us natives that

their 'clients' have a perfect right to live here. The ambition of multiculturalists is to take from the natives any right of refusal – or, more accurately, to take away from the natives any sense that they could ever be justified in thinking of exercising such a right. 'The United Kingdom', says the Parekh Report very solemnly, 'should formally declare itself to be a multi-cultural society' (Parekh, 2002: xxi). Britain's ethnic minorities, the multiculturalists tell us, are no longer small groups of guests of a majority host society (see below), but our co-inheritors, co-creators of Great Britain.

MULTICULTURE'S GRAND NARRATIVE

In the moral drama of humanity, ethnic minorities (who are mostly black or brown) are seen as the virtuous victims of a once-dominant, exploitative Western Empire, run by whites, for the benefit of whites, at the expense of everyone else. The grand narrative, therefore, consists of a historical drama that imputes moral cupidity and venality to the white West, its nation states and empires; confers, in and by contrast, redemptive decency on the one-time victims; and sees in their presence in the societies of the West little more than a just and necessary reparation for centuries of exploitation, degradation and misery. In the dramas of multiculturalism, the bad-mouthing of the West seems to be the necessary condition for the good-mouthing of the Rest.

INSTITUTIONALISED MULTICULTURALISM:
THE MULTICULTURAL ESTABLISHMENT

Multiculturalists are well established in British universities, trusts, research institutes and, increasingly, in the agencies of government. The expanded social science departments of the university system of the 1960s were well placed to respond to the growing public and political concern with 'race relations' and 'racism'. Some of the leading lights of multiculturalism are themselves members of ethnic minorities, ethnic 'faith groups', and ethnically based pressure groups. Many of them are involved with 'policy', appearing on government panels or influential 'think tanks', or in universities – indeed, often enough, the same people are to be found in a variety of settings, combining (for example) the stance of the academic with the style of the adviser, activist or policy maker. This network of institutional memberships and loyalties tends to make multiculturalists a particularly convinced or committed set of people: disinterest in their subject is not one of their characteristics. Their stock in trade is polemic. Much of the research and writings they produce is of high quality and high political visibility. Multicultural programmes and conferences, occasional seminars, annual and international events, cover a wide range of topics, and reinforce and extend the supportive friendship–peer networks. The media give ample coverage to these events and the literature they produce; and the media themselves are assiduous purveyors of the multicultural mission and grand narrative.

Multiculturalists are, then, an influential presence in the ruling stratum of British society. While multiculturalists are neither a conspiracy nor confessors of a creed, they do have a definite project, purpose, programme and ideology. While much of their research is, indeed, of high quality, it is generally deeply embedded in the moral and historical 'drama' I have tried to summarise above. There is such a thing as 'institutional multiculturalism', exemplified, perhaps, in the hostile comment tossed in my direction at one multicultural gathering that 'you are not one of us'. The ones that are 'of us' produce books, articles, web pages, documentaries, reports, etc., which are certainly 'relevant' to our contemporary concerns, but which, as polemic, tend to see a bit of a story as the whole of it. They are also, as already noted, somewhat uncritical of some of their own basic assumptions, carried away, perhaps, by the self-evident justice of the struggle against racism – though this, as I shall show, tends too often to degenerate into what is almost vulgar abuse of the (white) West. In this, at times, the multicultural house style is rather like that of the 'media', as described by John Lloyd in *What the Media are Doing to Our Politics* (Lloyd, 2004). Like the media, though with considerably higher motives, multiculturalists are engaged in a Long March through our institutions. Neither they nor the media are alone in this. Contemporary fiction, especially fiction written by members of ethno-religious minorities, is similarly and as obsessively concerned to 'critique' bourgeois white British society and its institutions. In this, literary fiction, in particular, can become a most self-indulgent thing. As one literary critic puts it, fiction, as it strays (as, like the media, it often does) from historical facts, causes 'historical reality to recede behind the rhetorical and narrative effects of [its] discourse' (Lassner, 2004: 5). In other words, treat it, and indeed the media and multiculturalism, with a pinch of salt.

The multicultural 'house style' and its political ambitions, pedigree and provenance can be very conveniently encountered in *The Future of Multi-Ethnic Britain, the Report of the Commission on the Future of Multi-Ethnic Britain*, published by Profile Books in 2000, and reissued in 2002. I will refer frequently to this book, known, after the chairman of the commission that produced it (Baron Parekh of Kingston upon Hull), as the Parekh Report. The Commission was set up in 1998 by the Runnymede Trust, an independent 'think-tank devoted to the cause of promoting racial justice in Britain'. The members of the Commission (all listed in the Report) are among the leading lights of British multiculturalism. Lord Parekh is a major author and academic in his own right, as is Professor Tariq Modood, the 'adviser' to the Commission. I will refer often to Professor Modood's work, too.

A relatively quick reading of the Parekh Report will illustrate my comments on 'mission statement' and 'grand narrative'. So, for example, the Parekh Report does not approve of the words 'majority' and 'minority'. Indeed, it refuses (or tries to refuse) to use them, seeing the word 'majority' as perpetuating 'the myth of white homogeneity', 'the non-existent homogeneous cultural structure of the "majority"', while 'minority' is seen as implying 'less important' or 'marginal', and being therefore 'insulting'. Similar concerns arise over the words 'ethnic', 'race' and 'black, Asian and Irish' (Parekh, 2002: x, xxiii–iv). Multiculturalists feel obliged to try to alter the very terms we use to describe humanity: new words will see off old words, ushering in new *worlds* – new and better, human, possibilities. There is, in all of this, a hint of the arrogance of the magician: utter the word, surrender the fact – which is quite a typical multicultural stance, especially when the words in question are those of the 'majority' and the surrendered words represent a real surrender.

While the 'majority' may not exist (a 'myth', not a fact, a 'false belief') (Parekh, 2002: 61), both in the Report and elsewhere it is, from time to time, re-created and, in keeping with the grand narrative, it comes in for considerable negative and nasty comment: the majority can exist when it has to be 'on call' to receive censure and reproof. No such danger applies to 'minorities', however, which retain the protection of non-existence, thus freeing them from such problems as being asked questions about their own possible responsibility for their position in society. Such discussion, says Lord Parekh very early on in his document, 'clearly falls outside the scope of this report' (Parekh, 2002: x). Minorities, as objects of possible critical comment, simply do not exist in the Parekh Report.

DIS-INVENTING THE MAJORITY: AN EXAMPLE

The negative view of, or even hostility to, the very idea of a 'majority' culture runs through most multicultural writing and speechmaking. This is particularly true when multiculturalists have to confront the conjunction of 'majority' and 'nation', as in 'the British nation' (or, worse, the 'English nation'). Often enough, this hostility is masked as mere 'factual' comment – as in what follows. As the first of seven trends that lie behind 'the unsettling of Britain', we read on page 23 of the Parekh Report:

> **Globalisation**
> The growing inter-dependence of the world's major regions results from the rapid movement of global capital and investment, deregulation of financial and other markets, the rise of multinational corporations, the spread of new information and communication technologies, the new cultural industries and global consumption patterns. One effect has been to weaken, though not yet fatally undermine, aspects of national

sovereignty, the nation-state as an exclusive political focus, national economies and the idea of nation as the guarantor of citizenship. There has been a corresponding growth in local and regional attachments ('glocalisation').

This is a clear case of the wish being father to the 'fact'. Surely nothing could be further from the truth? In one sense, 'globalisation' is a banality – saying nothing more than that we all live on the globe – where else?! Far from this fact leading to cheek-by-jowl global multicultural togetherness, we have seen in the twentieth century the human race separate itself out into more and more discrete, and often rival, exclusive political entities. The great majority – 97 per cent – of the world's people live and die in the same place as they were born (UN, 2003); and more of them are now born in, and stay in, nations. Empires (which *were* genuinely multicultural, though not egalitarian) have all gone, their passing regarded as a Good Thing by multiculturalists. The Great War destroyed several of the empires that went into it.

The League of Nations, which came into existence after 1919, had about 42 members, and, in 1945, 50 nation states signed up for and joined the United Nations. Now there are, by the most reliable count, 191 nation states, and probably more. This continues a process, accelerated by the Treaty of Versailles, whereby membership (willing or otherwise) of large political empires or small ethnic tribes has been superseded by membership of nation states. The most recent empire to collapse was, of course, the USSR. Over the lifetime of the United Nations, nation states have been created at the rate of about three a year. Bangladesh, for example, as East Pakistan, was once part of Pakistan, itself carved out of British India. The process is not over yet. Recently, we have seen large numbers of new nation states pop up in Central and Eastern Europe. There is no sign that this process has come to an end: a new one, Montenegro, came into existence last year.

These nation states are now *the* prime source and *locus* of civic loyalty, to an extent that they never were in the past. They are vociferously defensive about their sovereignty: time and again, international humanitarian efforts to intercede in their 'internal' affairs are rebutted on the grounds of 'sovereignty'. At the time of writing, 25 million people are 'refugees' *inside* their own states, held there by governments that keep them in as resolutely as they keep would-be humanitarian interveners out. The human race is now more politically differentiated than it has ever been. Global means different. I cannot now be a citizen of Kenya (where I grew up) *and* of the UK: I (and my wife, who was born in colonial Kenya) had to choose between the two. We chose to come home.

The governments of these newly invigorated nation states are more, not less, insistent on exclusive loyalty. The new nation states have absolutely no intention of being multicultural. They may (as we do) welcome guests, strangers, as tourists or workers of one kind or another; but they all have strong citizenship laws, brusque tests of loyalty and, usually, an insistence on political conformity. (In Chapter 7 I make some comment on India, a country that exemplifies many of the tensions caused by multiculturalism.) In many cases, the conformity sought by these new nation states is angry and adamant, enforced by police, army, prison, guns and, occasionally, by genocide or wholesale eviction – ethnic 'cleansing', not just in the 'Third World', but in our own continent, in our own time. God help us. The most shameful thing to have happened in Europe in the last 10 years was the massacre of thousands of Muslims by Serbs, all in the name of a Serbian nation state, and watched by Dutch soldiers over-respectful (to say the least) of the sovereignty of that state.

Inasmuch as people seeking asylum in the UK are concerned, if they are genuine (and not all are), they seek asylum precisely from such demands for political 'conformity'.

Tourists should, perhaps, be mentioned here as one of the 'new cultural industries' referred to by Lord Parekh. Hundreds of millions of people fly, drive or sail on holidays abroad every year. In both their numbers and their impact, they give rise to many of the mantras about 'the global village' or 'globalisation', or Parekh's 'weakening' of the nation state. Again, this is nonsense. Tourists are essentially in transit from one nation state to another. The simple business of flying aeroplanes or of sailing ships requires national accreditation of trained personnel and national enforcement of safety regulations. Such regulations may, indeed, be 'inter-national': this means precisely that they require competent national authorities to sign up to them. It is the competence and stability of both the exporting and the importing nation states that make tourism possible. Where nation states are incompetent, or failing, or dangerous, then they have no tourists, in or out, though they may well have mass murders, genocides and refugees. Most squabbling and failing nations are multicultural nations. Sensible tourism presupposes sensible nations. I might also point out that many tourists live in tourist colonies, often as segregated as old-style colonies ever were, with minimal multicultural contact (other than predatory) with the native population. In many places, the police and other paramilitary forces of the more nervous nation states regulate the boundaries of these new tourist colonies. Given the problems associated with the export and exhibition of white flesh and sex, which is what tourism often looks like, this is probably just as well. And tourists go home, leaving at least their money behind them.

Contrary to what Lord Parekh and his Commission believe, nation states are not fading way: they are proliferating and becoming less, not more, tolerant of divergent and competing loyalties. As I said above, Parekh's claims are clear examples of the wish becoming father to the 'fact'.

A MULTICULTURAL WORLD?

What reasons are *we* offered as to why something (multiculturalism) that is hemlock to most of the members of the United Nations (United *Nations*, note) should be regarded as honey for Britain? As I indicated above, one of the reasons why multiculturalism is urged upon us is, it is said, that we, after centuries of exploitation of the black and brown people of the world, owe something to them; we are simply repaying a debt, covering with decent clothes what David Dabydeen calls the 'pornography of Empire' (Stein, 2004: 152). Chapter 3 deals at some length with the subject of the Empire.

In addition to that, if we reject multiculturalism we run the risk (as something which is our fault) of becoming 'unsettled', 'narrow' and 'unstable': the word 'decline' or one of its synonyms, applied to Britain, occurs 17 times in a single 17-line paragraph on page 25 of the Parekh Report. Somewhat illogically, we are simultaneously urged to consider that the societies of 'old' Europe, including Britain, are (unlike so many others) so hugely stable as to be able both to be welcoming and to flourish with an extraordinary variety of cultures and values, including (in our case) between 300,000 and 500,000 illegal immigrants and associated folk, whose existence is making our governmental structures look ridiculous. As an example of such an illogical demand that we be both unsettled and stable, a strange protestation, we have the *Independent* of 31 March 2006. Under the headline 'IMMIGRATION: The Facts we are Never Told', the newspaper quotes Home Office estimates (*sic*) of between 310,000 and 570,000 illegal immigrants in the UK. The *Independent* took the line that, if all these were legalised, there would be an immediate boost in, for example, the tax revenue of the Treasury, a saving in police costs, less hassle all round, etc. We, presumes the *Independent*, need such immigrants as fellow citizens.

One such exemplary immigrant, given us by the *Independent* as evidence, I assume, *for* their argument, was 'Charles'. The paragraph below is a *précis* of the *Independent*'s biography of Charles: Charles had come into Britain from Brazil on false pretences (allegedly to visit his mother); had paid £500 for false work papers ('made in London very quickly', said Charles), another £100 for a false national insurance certificate, paid another £200 to a fraudulent employment agency, and through them worked illegally until picked up by the Immigration services and deported.

Charles, who had lied his way into Britain, and lied on his journeys while in it, and lied to get work, told the *Independent* that he felt 'betrayed, cheated and robbed'. I know how he feels.

Charles, one assumes, might feel that his 'human rights' had been assailed. The *Independent* would appear to support him in this view. More sensibly, perhaps, it might be felt that

Charles demonstrates very clearly that human beings cannot, and should not, be trusted with human rights.

In presenting us with such a case for sympathy, the *Independent* would seem to expect us to be, at one and the same time, properly full of remorse for what 'we' have 'done' to people like Charles; to accept the 'narrowness', unfairness and instability of our own insular little society; and yet, by opening our borders to very large numbers of such Charleses and others, to behave as if we are unproblematically possessed of a social and political stability known practically nowhere else. Should we ourselves advance a claim to such stability, we should, of course, immediately be accused of the multicultural offence of 'triumphalism'. How intriguing: the very stability on which ethnic minority residents rely, and to which billions of others aspire, becomes an offence, unless it is of advantage to migrants, to whom its existence, as 'triumphalism', is offensive!

HOW IS SOCIETY POSSIBLE?

The question of social stability – 'how is society possible?' – is the most fundamental of all socio-political questions. If we are, indeed, a successful society and a stable state, then we are so because we are mono- and not multicultural. Most of the other countries of the world would seem to take the same view. Contrary to the 'we are all global villagers' ideology, if other countries are stable and successful it is because they work at establishing a central, nation-based core value, to which all citizens are expected to adhere. Many of these countries, as, for example, (British) India, were at Independence very genuinely, and very troublingly, multicultural: partition was one solution. In Chapter 7, I will try to show how persistent is the effort in modern India to create an exclusive sense of nationality. India has that lesson for us – as well as other lessons about the political and social problems embedded in multiculturalism.

In considering the matter of the capacity of British society to absorb the attitudes and values of a multiplicity of ethno-religious minorities, we need to consider, obviously enough, the matter of our own 'culture'. If we indeed view the question of 'culture' in the traditional sense – that is, of the level of civilisation exemplified in an active elite, properly defining, redefining, propagating *and exemplifying* public moral codes – then there are strong grounds for believing that British society is in meltdown: too many of our citizens seem to have decided to become stupid. To be absolutely clear, this is in no way the 'fault' of post-war immigrants: we did it our way. We have the rags and tatters of a once competent culture.

We also, however, have the institutional means, as well as the tradition, of digging ourselves out of such holes of our own making. It is precisely these means, the institutions of our civil society and associated political systems, that are being corrupted by policies and programmes urged on us by multiculturalism. In this context, when multiculturalists say that our national culture is in decline – something with which many of us would agree – they mean, in effect, that the decline is somehow liberating or necessary – and I do not agree with that. Furthermore, they fail to see that a crucial part of our non-homogeneous non-majority culture consists of tried and tested methods of dealing with problems of social and economic change; and that these are very clearly rooted in a national majority culture, inherited as a task in hand, not a finished product. *These social and political mechanisms are precisely what make an apparent lack of homogeneity possible.* These methods do not include privileged access to politicians, the circumscription of speech, subsidised special pleading, etc. They *certainly* do not include bombs on London buses, burning books, subverting or attacking the police or the armed forces, rioting to close a theatre, or cheating at elections.

Crucially, such systems of practical politics require a fundamental loyalty to this country: not because it is perfect, but precisely because it is not. We do need to think very carefully about the costs of adding new groups or new religions to Britain, and about the particular values and behaviour of the groups or religions that have arrived here. Contrary to another of the ideological premises of multiculturalism, *they are not all the same.* Some are useful, benign and *simpatico*;

others are not. There is as little sense in being asked 'Are you for or against multiculturalism?' as there is in being asked 'Are you for or against bricks?' As any bricklayer would tell you, and as any visitor to a brickyard will realise, there are hundreds of different kinds of bricks, of all shapes, sizes, colours and load-bearing capacities. It all depends on what you want the bricks for.

No more do all minorities come from 'parent' cultures seriously committed, as we are asked to be, to liberal multiculturalism. In Muslim Afghanistan, a convert to Christianity can be saved from being beheaded only by pleading insanity. In Hindu India, an Australian missionary and his two sons were, in 1999, burned alive by a Hindu mob: Graham Staines had been working in a leper colony for 30 years. The Hindu mob just killed him. Christian worshippers have been killed in Pakistan and Egypt. Jamaica's own government thinks the country is on a slide into crime and anarchy. Sikhs and Hindus fought each other in India, and Sikhs staged a very effective riot at a theatre in Birmingham. And we, so determined to be liberal in the face of this, can so twist our minds as to somehow make us as nasty too, the pot and the kettle agreeing to call each other black, as it were. In a rather astonishing paragraph, and in a book otherwise quite hostile to multiculturalism, we read: 'Many assume that religious extremism is a characteristic solely of Islam. The massacre of some 30,000 Jews and Muslims in 1099 by Christian Crusader extremists illustrates that it is not' (West, 2005: 62). The verbs are, as you will notice, all in the present tense.

We should think beyond the invented cosmeticised collectivities presented to us by multicultural apologists: there are nasty as well as nice Hindus, and there are law-wrecking as well as law-abiding Jamaicans. Ultimately, the issue of 'social justice' is better dealt with through the creative fictions and palpable realities of traditional British individualism than through the stultifying categories of our multiculturalists. Amongst such traditions are those of good manners, including those defining the respective duties and responsibilities of hosts and guests. In the early days of post-war immigration, much was heard of such a model of behaviour. Such a model certainly has its limits; but they are not, to my mind, as difficult to live with as the angry distance of strangers, which multiculturalism has helped create.

HOSTS AND GUESTS

A host creates a space and a place into which he invites guests. He does not, while creating it, have any particular guests in mind. He does not, of course, have to invite anyone at all. Implicit in his invitation is the prior right of possession and ownership vested in the host. He has built, or owns, or has annexed, the place to which he chooses to invite his guests. His guests are there as the result of an invitation, not 'as of right'. Guests remain guests so long as they conform to certain standards of 'guest-ship'. These standards are those of the host, not of the guest; and the host, but not the guest, has the right to vary them. All guest-ness is conditional; the conditions are defined by the host. Any host of competence knows that he should choose guests compatible with his own house style, and with the comfort and welfare of other guests, should there be any.

Presence in the host's house in no way confers upon the guest a right of residence. Indeed, it confers upon the guest a due and careful obligation to educate himself in the terms of the hospitality of which he is the beneficiary; to ensure that he and such of his dependants as might be with him, i.e. those who have been invited by the host, abide by those terms – it is the guest's responsibility to ensure that they do. It is taken as 'understood' that the presence in the host's domain of the guest is a temporary presence. The guest should know when to go. This, in itself, is no diminution of the pleasure to be derived from the encounter, which is seen as being, quite properly, both temporary and, at the time, inegalitarian – to be reciprocated, perhaps, at some future date. The guest should leave when the host so indicates, and the guest is obliged to school himself in the subtle ways in which these indications to leave are expressed. It is no part of the job of the host to ensure that the guest has a proper domicile to which to return. If there is an emergency – say, if the guest's house burns down while he is at the house of the host – then the host may (*may*) offer extended, conditional hospitality.

No 'third party' exists, or can be invoked, to moderate the relationships between host and guest, and certainly not to confer upon the guest any right that might, in its exercise, qualify or diminish the rights of the host. The host is expected to be as polite as the guest, and to make his substance available to the guest in a generous and cheerful way, free of all expectations of return or reward. True, gratitude, in the main, flows one way – from the guest to the host, though no proper host would assume the right to demand such gratitude, and roles may, of course, be reversed at some time in the future. Guests who 'sing for their supper' offer, in so doing, a gift to the host for his hospitality. Should friction arise between guest and host, or unpleasantness occur, then relationships are simply broken off, at the initiative of either host or guest. Indeed, such an action by the guest is his main, if not only, sanction: he or she goes, resulting in both parties then becoming strangers to one another. A friend of mine, who is lightly and not very obviously 'black', was a guest at dinner one evening when the host and others began to express ideas about racism being a good thing. She simply got up, said that she felt unable to continue to sit at such a table, and left, together with her husband. Of course, she may well have left behind her a host free (freer, even) to articulate his obnoxious views further; on the other hand, such a well-mannered put-down may have been a rebuttal much more effective than a stern finger-wagging from the Race Relations Board, or some such. Guests and hosts relate to each other as individuals – there are few occasions for collective, 'umpired' relationships.

A guest's main 'freedom to choose' is circumscribed by the potential attraction to his host of other, alternative, guests. The same applies to hosts. Both need to make themselves attractive, the host to the guest, the guest to the host.

The term 'the host community' was used quite frequently in the early days of post-war immigration, with little embarrassment in its use – quite the opposite. Hosts were not hard to find, English people, at most social levels, being generally polite.

Clergymen were, indeed are, often among the most active of hosts, offering and supporting newcomers to a cold and strange land. The Christian religion, indeed the Judeo-Christian religion, is very aware of the desirability of looking after widows, orphans and 'the stranger that is within your gate'. Indeed, for a couple of decades, 'inter-communal' and 'inter-faith' relations were almost interchangeable, with many an Anglican minister only too willing to ascribe equal theological status to other monotheistic religions 'of the book', or spiritual status at least to religious practices which had a colour and vibrancy missing from their own liturgies and formularies. Thus, for example, Rowan Williams, looking back on encountering Muslims reading their scriptures:

> We Christians were able to benefit enormously from
> watching Muslims do what Muslims do with love,
> intellectual rigour and excitement. It proved a
> deeper and more truly respectful meeting of minds
> than any attempt to find a neutral common ground..
> (Ipgrave, 2004: 140)

Universities, at national and local level, provided congenial members of the various 'Race Relations' boards, including the later SACREs (religious education committees), which administered or provided guidelines for religious education. Universities, of course, provided an ample reservoir of secularists; and for these, too, immersion in 'race' or 'community' relations could be seen as promoting a pluralist, less nationalistic and more 'tolerant' vision of British society and its educational and political practices.

The Labour Party, drawing on its international tradition, also provided 'hosts', and was an important element in facilitating the opening of housing, schools and other social services to immigrants and their families. For reasons that may or may not endure, Britain's ethnic minorities, where they have indicated a political preference, whether in voting or in party membership, tend at the moment to be Labour supporters. In a way this is odd, as the entrepreneurial attitudes expressed in the lifestyle of many ethnic minorities are not on all fours with Labourist ideas. However, at least for the time being, the political 'host' tends to be the Labour Party.

At moments of crisis, these various members of the 'local squirearchy' would offer moral and actual support to our guests. If I may be allowed a personal note: when the Rushdie Affair was at its height, and Muslims in Bradford, thwarted in their expressed desire to kill Mr Rushdie, were instead burning his books, Muslim leaders in Newcastle were seeking support both for their views on Rushdie and for a petition to change the law on blasphemy so as to protect Islam. As a local (Labour) councillor, and a university lecturer in Religious Studies, I was involved (at some unimportant level) in these discussions. It was clear then that mollifying noises from people like me, and from other non-Muslim parties to the discussion, were already calling into question the 'host–guest relationship'. Muslim representatives could simply not accept our views that God (or, if you prefer, Allah) was big enough to look after himself: this somewhat Anglican stance was unacceptable. Our expressed disinclination to burn books or effigies of Mr Rushdie, still less the man himself, was not persuasive, either. What was good enough for the host was not good enough for the guest, and the house rules had – the young Muslim said in effect – to change. Fifteen years or so later, of course, the guest, in the bill covering 'Incitement to Religious Hatred', seems to have won. The chief host, the prime minister, told BBC radio on 12 April 2005 that the (lapsed) bill would be reintroduced in order 'to placate the Muslim community'; and Sir Iqbal Sacranie, secretary of the Muslim Council of Britain, commented that it had taken some time to persuade the government to bring in the bill, and that the government should not 'play dirty politics' with the legislation (BBC Radio 4, 10 April 2005). The host did as he was told. The guest now determines the quality of the table linen.

Sir Iqbal Sacranie, of course, is now one of that number of spokesmen to whom hosts must now feel *obliged* to issue invitations: the host has lost the initiative. Indeed, the host begins to feel guilty at being the host in the first place. It is a superordinate position in a society insistent on the impropriety of its concomitant – subordination. Institutionalised multiculturalism has arrived in Britain.

CONCLUSION

While more could be said about guests and hosts, such a stylised set of relationships is clearly no longer (if it ever was) acceptable to multiculturalists as a template for inter-ethnic encounters. Contemporary multiculturalism now has little truck with such notions, perhaps finding them altogether too bland and devoid of ideological 'thrust'. They are also, of course, too firmly located in the 'voluntary' sphere of civil society, unavailable to the top-down regulatory condescension of firm government. I conclude this opening chapter with comments on two aspects of the contemporary multicultural 'discourse'.

Firstly, we are talking about multicultural 'spokesmen' or 'spokeswomen' for those ethnic minorities who have arrived here since World War Two. Frequently enough (and to my mind speciously), earlier 'immigrants' or 'minorities', such as the Welsh or the Irish Catholics or the Jews, are portrayed by multiculturalists as if they were some kind of precedent, some sort of home-grown minority. They are – but not in the way seen by multiculturalists. I am Welsh, a member of a minority. That fact, on its own, gives me very little in common with Hindus from Tamil Nadu or Muslims from the Punjab.

Secondly, I have little idea as to how 'representative' multiculturalists are of the ethnic minorities they claim to represent. Like most academics and intellectuals, they usually follow well behind, or run too far ahead, of the field they pretend to lead, and are unaware of this ludicrous position. There are some multiculturalists who are now beginning to sense that their imposition on black and brown people of a collective 'minority' or 'victim' status is itself experienced by them as stigmatising and even dangerous. Even more problematic for these lately wise people, as well as for the rest of us, is the realisation that their persistent and deliberate defamation of the majority culture is building up a backlash waiting to happen.

In the last chapter, 'Multicultural Collapse', I will deal with the latest twists in multiculturalism, as it endeavours to face up to a 'multicultural' ferocity it neither predicted nor understands. I refer, of course, to bombing all over the world, and, in particular, to the bombing of London trains and buses by British-born Muslims. That one event in London confounds the silly idea that being born British in itself makes you British. Bombs are a difficult form of 'dialogue' to encompass within the multicultural mindset; yet, as far as I can see, it is as 'dialogue' that these bombs have (astonishingly enough) been classified by an, admittedly, chastened multicultural Establishment.

Their main concern, though, after the London bombings, and the promise of more, was to catalogue and deplore instances of 'Islamophobia', telling us how insecure the *Muslim* community felt! This seemed to me to be another example of how, in spite of such horrors as the London bombings, multiculturalists sail on regardless, insisting on the prior and continuing validity of their vocabulary of 'discrimination' and 'injustice'. This view continues to have force as the necessary intellectual underpinning of various programmes of 'positive discrimination' and 'racial justice', the full impact of which we are yet to feel. Multiculturalists possess, even in doubt, a proclamatory ideology, grounded in the notion of Human Rights and in a version of that self-hating and self-abasing tradition of Western anti-Westernism known as 'occidentalism'. Multiculturalists are not so resolutely *multi* as to be able to say many good things about the West. They are quick to identify what they consider to be acts of 'discrimination' (always wrong), and to demand action by legislature or judiciary to outlaw or punish the discriminator. More radical are the demands for employment 'targets' for black and brown people, and then, as sure as night follows day, for quotas and positive discrimination in organisations like the police, universities and the army. They see the arrival of ethnic minorities in the UK, France, Germany, etc. not only as the actual exercise of Human Rights, but also as a perfectly proper settling of imperial scores and accounts, the determined and triumphant 'return' of the one-time colonially repressed.

At the beginning of 2006, a young civil servant told a regional gathering that the North East was economically backward because it was 'hideously white' (a label initially applied, it seems, not to us Geordies, but rather, and apparently without demur, by Mr Greg Dyke to his colleagues at the BBC). The ease of recourse to such insulting language (now worn with pride on T-shirts in the North East) indicates one of the several sub-promotional themes of British multiculturalism – the persistent (and increasingly successful) effort to inculcate in the white majority a sense of their own moral ignominy and 'ethnic' unfitness. So pervasive is, or should be, this ignominy, this unfitness, that it is held to vastly circumscribe, if not totally vitiate, whatever claim we (the hideously white) might make to the exclusive occupation of these islands. It is to this issue that I now turn.

CHAPTER 2

NATION STATE: *DO* THE BRITISH EXIST?

This chapter could well be passed over by those to whom the question 'Do the British exist?' is just too silly to be of interest.

As any attitude survey or opinion poll shows, the British are quite well aware that they exist. Unfortunately, multiculturalists are as keen as any Marxist used to be to deny the reality of 'nation' or 'people', to deny that there is any such thing as Britain. This does not, of course, stop them from proceeding to the task invoked by the title of the next chapter: once multiculturalists have decided that we do not exist, it then becomes necessary to re-create us so as to be able to ascribe to us all sorts of dire responsibilities for crimes, genocides and global rapine, as well as a generalised incompetence. We thus exist, at least as an object of censure and vilification; but only, obviously, so that we can then be re-abolished. This is the subject of the next chapter: 'We are the Fascists who won – Should Britain Exist?'

DO THE BRITISH EXIST?

> Citizenship has been well defined as the right
> ordering of our several loyalties.
> > (Hadow, 1923: 1)

> If Englishness does not define me, then redefine
> Englishness.
> > (Andrea Levy, in Stein, 2004: 17)

> An Englishman born and bred, almost.
> > (Kureishi, 1990: 3)

All individuals have equal worth irrespective of their colour, gender, ethnicity, religion, age or sexual orientation.

(Parekh, 2002: xiii)

If Rights are all that matter, and all Rights are *Human* Rights, then there is no moral or legal justification for that form of exclusivity which a nation, simply, is. While, to my mind, nothing but the most ludicrously amiable social confusion would arise by trying to ignore, in any form of sociability, the attributes listed immediately above by Lord Parekh, I can see that, from such an unreal premise, all human beings – everywhere, any time, in any country to which fate may have delivered them – have an equal right to anything that is going; and where there is *any* infringement of such rights – where, for example, one individual has less broccoli, or less access to jobs or education, or to diamonds, or to a bus pass, than any other individual – then injustice arises. Human Rights, being human, need no passport and are duty free.

To be fair, Lord Parekh goes on to say that 'individuals' (he somewhat disingenuously slips in the word 'citizen') are not only just individuals, but are 'members of particular religious, ethnic, cultural and regional communities'. Even here, though, he is able to avoid mention of 'nation', because for him it does not really exist. He refers, as above, to 'the nonexistent homogeneous cultural structure of the "majority"'. Then he castigates those 'academics and other specialists' who have assisted policy makers in espousing and propagating the 'myth of homogeneity – the false belief that the population of Britain consists essentially of one large majority or mainstream ("white people") and an array of various minorities' (Parekh, 2002: 61). Within this 'sociological' framework, in which a non-existent majority confronts the overarching supremacy of Human Rights, multiculturalists are able to regard W. H. Hadow's maxim, quoted at the beginning of this section, as of little relevance. They are, as I shall try to demonstrate, wrong: Hadow is right. Still, as Dervla Murphy puts it in Modood (1992): 'If you know nothing about a people, you can believe anything.'

Defoe is often mobilised as an early, if somewhat sardonic, multiculturalist:

The *Romans* first with *Julius Caesar* came,
Including all the Nations of that Name,
Gauls, *Greeks* and *Lombards*; and by Computation,
Auxiliaries or Slaves of ev'ry Nation.
With *Hengist*, *Saxons*; *Danes* with *Sueno* came,
In search of Plunder, not in search of Fame.
Scots, *Picts* and *Irish* from th' Hibernian Shore
And Conq'ring *William* brought the *Normans* o'er.
All these their Barb'rous Offspring left behind,
The Dregs of Armies, they of all Mankind;
Blended with *Britons* who before were here,
Of whom the *Welsh* ha' blest the Character.
From this Amphibious Ill-born Mob began
That vain ill-natur'd thing, an Englishman.
(Daniel Defoe, *The English Race*)

In this poem, Defoe provides a pedigree of sorts for the English – an 'ill-born mob, that vain ill-natur'd thing' – a cheerfully caustic comment on claims of genetic or cultural homogeneity or hegemony.

With Bede, we learnt about the early stages of the formation of the (Christian) English nation. When the leader of a predatory and itinerant band of Angles (*rex anglorum*) proclaimed himself King of England (*rex angliae*), neither he nor anyone else would, or could, possibly have seen himself as the progenitor, by 2006, of the *United Kingdom of Great Britain and Northern Ireland*. Still less could he have imagined that, amongst his titular descendants, would be those claiming ('*By the Grace of God*') to be, amongst other extraordinary things, '*Empress of India, Defender of the Faith, Queen of Canada, Australia, and of her other Realms and Territories, Head of the Commonwealth*'. It is difficult to see how any Saxon, Celt or Pict could ever have imagined that from this wet and boggy island would come an extraordinary and extensive imperial force. Still less, even, would he have imagined how successfully his descendants managed to survive the loss of their empire and their global dominance.

In laying exclusive claim for himself and his fellow tribesmen to occupation of a finite piece of earth ('England'), this tribal leader made his contribution to the creation of a nation – the nation to which I, and perhaps you, belong.

As it happens, I am Welsh. My paternal grandfather was a founder member of Plaid Cymru. As a boy I used to sing, in Welsh, 'Land of My Fathers', about 'my country tho' crushed by a hostile array' and 'Men of Harlech', in which 'Onward comes the Saxon foe. . .a Saxon life shall pay.' A famous 1817 painting by John Martin, *The Bard,* shows how graphically these sentiments can be expressed: the Bard in question stands high on the crag above the cataract, raining curses down on the conquering English army filing through the river gorge below: then, as tradition has it, the Bard hurls himself down into the abyss in a kind of suicidal revenge: 'Ruin seize thee ruthless King: confusion on thy banners wait', as Thomas Gray puts it. As a small boy, I used to join with other small boys in thumping Geraint Thomas, who said that the progress of the English armies into North Wales had been made possible by Welsh quislings and by Welsh labourers who sold themselves and their country to earn a living on the building sites of the English castles. Geraint suffered for his apostasy. On the battlefields of North Wales, or indeed of Culloden or the Boyne, I knew (and know) which 'side' I am on. Not for nothing are the songs of the Celts exercises in lachrymose, defeated, bitter and well-adjusted nostalgia. My wife, though, is English, and my sons support the English rugby team.

These old stories may well be, now, for most of us Celts even, histories with no purpose, though not (to most of us Celts) without meaning. They are, though, the *shared* slowly worked-out inheritance of Celts with others – Saxons, Normans, Danes, and indeed with others not always co-resident with us. *Over several centuries*, this slow and often painful process – a pain that is never equally distributed – resulted in a successful, competent and creative nation state, a national culture. This is not something to be picked over lightly in some kind of multicultural jumble sale, or regarded as constituting a type of permanent invitation to all and sundry to come to add yet another chapter to the 'mongrel nation'. After 1,400 years of strife and truce, the 'terms of settlement' of Mercians, Angles, Saxons and Jutes, of Danes and Normans, as well as of the various branches of the aboriginal Celts, came to substantial practical closure about 300 years ago, after which we British have been able to construct a real and distinct nation. To be sure, Huguenots came to Britain, as did Irish Catholics and Russian-Polish Jews, and no doubt many others; but they came here as minorities obliged to become one with the majority. They came as labourers, refugees or suppliants, stayed as guests (see above), and only, over many difficult decades and shared dangers, became fellow citizens in almost the same way that I, with *not one* of my ancestors born outside these islands, am.

> Britain is not and never has been the unified,
> conflict-free land of popular imagination. There is
> no single white majority.
>
> (Parekh, 2002: 26)

What, other than the very obvious ideological one, is the point of such comments? Nations are slow, stuttering and unsteady inventions, pieces of land to which a section of humanity attaches itself, by increments, claiming it for exclusive possession. Part of the 'licence' of possession is rooted in the proclamation of a common racial or genetic ancestry. Whether this section of humanity is, or can claim to be, 'really' genetically or racially homogeneous is one important factor, but not the only one. Nations become such by wrapping both natality and territoriality in a complexity of symbols – narratives, histories, language, ornament, religion, music, architecture, triumph, sorrows, humour – of which each successive generation is the exclusive inheritor and to each of which it adds. Natality and territoriality are among the basic ingredients of nationality; but then so are poems, songs, smells, games and jokes. Norman Tebbit's cricket test is nothing like as precise as the test of who laughs, and how they laugh, and who does not laugh, at 'Irish' jokes. This, of course, leaves aside the larger question of whether someone from Uttaranchal or Sulawesi would know or care what an 'Irish' joke was.

The processes of nation-making are neither steady nor necessarily all in one straight line. Wars (victorious or otherwise) and other dramas can either retard or promote plans and ambitions. A 'planned nation' is a rarity. Nations can become less than they once were, or can disappear altogether in the middle of being formed. A census of all the nations that have ever existed would probably show that most of them have indeed failed and/or disappeared – the Iceni and the Mohicans were not the only ones to go, and they will not be the last. The survival of those that persist or flourish, and how they do so, is a matter of very great interest. Success is never to be taken for granted, and is always to be wondered at.

As far as Britain is concerned, it is important to notice that the processes and periods of constructing a national identity in Britain are not coterminous with the construction of British democracy. The first general election to be held in Britain on the basis of universal adult (21 plus) suffrage took place in 1929. Only after 1966 did every citizen over the age of 18 acquire a vote. None of the early 'minorities' (Jews, Irish, Welsh, etc.) referred to immediately above joined a society that was under 'democratic' control. No more did they ask for special treatment – exemption from the basic rules, rather than the application of those rules to them. I will return to this point in later chapters.

As for nation and democracy, and war, nothing that I know of can match Abraham Lincoln's 271-word summation of these matters:

> Four score and seven years ago our fathers brought
> forth on this continent, a new nation, conceived in
> Liberty, and dedicated to the proposition that all men
> are created equal.
>
> Now we are engaged in a great civil war, testing
> whether that nation, or any nation so conceived or so
> dedicated, can long endure. We are met on a great

battlefield of that war. We have come to dedicate a portion of that field, as a final resting place for those who here gave their lives that that nation might live. It is altogether fitting and proper that we should do this.

But, in a larger sense, we can not dedicate – we can not consecrate – we can not hallow – this ground. The brave men, living and dead, who struggled here, have consecrated it, far above our poor power to add or detract. The world will little note, nor long remember what we say here, but it can never forget what they did here. It is for us the living, rather, to be dedicated here to the unfinished work which they who fought here have thus far so nobly advanced. It is rather for us to be here dedicated to the great task remaining before us – that from these honoured dead we take increased devotion to that cause for which they gave the last full measure of devotion – that we here highly resolve that these dead shall not have died in vain – that this nation, under God, shall have a new birth of freedom – and that government of the people, by the people, for the people, shall not perish from the earth.

I feel unable to add much to this. If you feel that more is needed, then please turn to Garry Wills' *Lincoln at Gettysburg: the Words that Remade America*. I may, though, be permitted three comments. First, Lincoln refers to 'all men', but he is clear that for 'all men' to have life and rights, then a nation must both exist and be a moral force. He knew that something that is held to inhere in everyone in fact inheres in no one: there may well be 'human' rights but no human outside the state will have them. Secondly, we hear Lincoln clearly saying here that a national inheritance is neither fixed nor unchanging – but that it is, nonetheless, real and compelling. He refers to the past, to the foundational act of America; then to the present, to the war; and then to the future, 'the great task remaining before us'. The 'us' is the American people, the American nation. Thirdly, well aware – on a civil war battlefield how could he not be? – that the dead that lay around him were not all of one mind, he invokes a powerful and transcendent loyalty, a proper obligation when a nation stands as representative of its own highest ideals. It is to *loyalty* that he appeals, not to some narrow fixity of race or space, but to the purpose, the task of enlisting the energies of his people in the business of making *this* place, *this* space, *this* nation, a decent and proper place in which to live. And it is on the battlefield, and from the battle-dead, that he drew his inspiration, knowing full well how difficult a road lay ahead. Nation-making is a steep and rugged pathway, not a stroll by the River Eden. I cannot sympathise overmuch with Tariq Modood's problems:

> It's not easy being British: in articles, papers and reviews over the last few years Tariq Modood has documented some of the main problems. It is not easy to identify the values, processes and customs which are distinctively British; not easy, having identified them, to be in all respects proud, grateful and loyal; not easy to be recognised and accepted fully by other people who are British; not easy to establish and protect public policies and laws which recognise and rejoice that there are many different ways of being British.
> (Modood, 1992: Preface by Robin Richardson, director of the Runnymede Trust)

There is, of course, no reason at all why it should be easy for Mr Modood or anyone else. The Chief Rabbi tells us to:

> Speak to our ideals, not to our interests, tell us the stories that unite us as a nation.
> (Chief Rabbi Jonathan Sacks, BBC Radio 4 'Thought for the Day', 6 December 2005)

This is not simply an Anglo-European predilection, for Bernard Lewis quotes a group of Arab leaders:

> Whoever lives in our country, speaks our language,
> is brought up in our culture *and takes pride in our*
> *glory is one of us.*
>
> (Lewis 1970: 9–10, my emphasis)

'Pride in our glory' is as good a definition of loyalty as I can imagine. It is to national ideals that we owe our loyalty, and from them that we derive it. This is not a strutting, bragging thing. Political loyalty is the obligation to want the best for the society into which you are born, or of which you wish to be part. This is not easy. There is, as Burke put it, a contract between the generations that were, that are, and that are yet to come. Loyalty exists when you feel ashamed of something evil or stupid done in the name of the nation of generations to which you belong. This is not easy. You are obliged, on such occasion, both to be ashamed and to do something about it. Loyalty does not demand perfection or a zero-blemish society. Disloyalty is the denial or discarding of that sense of obligation, or even the withdrawal of your energies and their application on behalf of some other collectivity, some other 'birthright'. None of this is easy. It would not be worth having if it was.

All babies, and all foreigners, are born or arrive without loyalty: they have to achieve and earn a birthright, assisted (or frustrated) in this by the 'bred in the bone' adults surrounding them. It is not enough to be, as Hanif Kureishi's character Karam Amir puts it when he describes himself as 'an Englishman born and bred, almost' (see above). Being 'almost' *is* easy.

By being ignorant, deliberately or otherwise, of the political community of which you are part, you run the risk of becoming disloyal. Part of political loyalty is the requirement to become familiar with the practical political tradition that puts bread in your mouth, pavements under your feet, stability and security around you, and hope in your children's hearts. While all of these things may be human rights, they are most evidently not the typical human experience. All of us should be aware of that. In particular, foreigners, immigrants, asylum seekers, would-be citizens – coming here, usually entirely voluntarily, from parts of the world where neither the theoretical rights nor the actuality are much in evidence – should consider very, very carefully how, here, these minor mundane miracles have come about. So should our children. So should we.

For 'outsiders' of one type or another, those not born into it, the fundamental meaning of this inheritance is relatively opaque, unavailable, perhaps, in the short term. 'Outsiders' seeking to understand – let alone become – 'insiders' have a very hard – *a properly and necessarily hard* – task in front of them: easy access is a fraud; instant access a dangerous delusion. There are no rights to inheritance; only obligations to earn it – day by day, day after day.

To repeat: all nations are unfinished business, always requiring making and remaking. This in no way means that they are vague nullities, capricious, malleable, without boundaries, untrue and unreal. In a real sense, the people of a nation claim exclusive possession of a finite piece of land because they are, or consider themselves to be, a virtuous community. Land is, by its nature, without moral status, its occupation as much the result of accident as of design. Yet title to that land comes to be vested in moralised natalities, ancestors, genetic or adopted, racial or symbolic ('ethnic' is now the politically correct term, but *only* for minorities – majorities insisting on ethnicity are 'racialist'). Together, ancestry and land, wrapped in a moral pedigree, constitute (for better or for worse) who we are.

The pedigree defines, *per contra*, who we are not: it identifies strangers or aliens. These are the parameters of loyalty.

Some aliens are enemies. There are, even now, in the Indian Ocean, sparsely populated islands whose inhabitants simply kill on sight anyone from outside: *all* their aliens are enemies. While all nations define and defend their boundaries, few are now as adamantly exclusive as these islanders. Not so long ago, my father in Bomber Command was engaged in the business of sending aeroplanes across borders to kill Germans. Italians were trying to kill my Uncle Dewi. At that time, Germans and Italians were considered by us to be both alien and hostile. Such patterns of enmity change, so that what my father did (not that long ago) is unthinkable, incomprehensible even, to my children: Germans might be aliens, but they are no longer enemies to be killed. They are even allies, friends. (Oddly, our wars seem to have conscripted more friends than enemies: war and multiculturalism will be dealt with later.)

Our national boundaries are now more open than they have been in the past. This is, in part, because we have lost both the inclination and the means to defend them. Devices such as the European Union and the Schengen accord formalise this fluidity, as does a general trend to facilitate practices such as the ownership and settlement by, say, non-Slovak citizens in ex-communist Slovakia, or the toleration by the French of the purchase by British citizens of tens of thousands of houses in France, where Englishmen can even become mayors in French villages. While neither ownership nor residence necessarily confers citizenship, it would seem that the adamance of the insistence on exclusive ownership and exclusive occupation of the land that has historically characterised the life of a nation is, in Europe anyway, weakening. (The extraordinary peculiarity of Europe, in this and other respects, will be dealt with later in this book.)

Related to such devices as the Schengen accord are facilities for humanitarian treatment of another type of alien called 'asylum seekers'. Such aliens have, of course, long been a feature of British national life, where they are secure and welcome in our land both because of their own need and because of our strength and stability and decency. The assumption is that such people are here (and are welcome here) until such time as the conditions in their homeland that forced them to leave are sorted out. At that point they will return to their own country; they are here temporarily, with neither rights nor expectation of permanent residence or citizenship. The benefit of their presence is mostly one way – from us, to them, with recompense to us being neither sought nor found. Substantial changes have taken place both in the numbers and nature of asylum seekers – another example, perhaps, of a real change being camouflaged as just 'more of the same' – yet the very existence of the legal category of 'asylum seekers' underscores the essential exclusivity of the occupation of this land by us, the British. It avoids the nonsense of categorising all aliens as enemies, to be excluded or killed, but without imposing on us any obligation to absorb even 'good' aliens into our national culture. Indeed, 'good' asylum seekers are the ones who go home. They are very close indeed to being the 'guests' referred to in the first chapter.

Things get more complicated when we consider the case of incomers, temporary or otherwise, whose presence is beneficial to themselves, to us, and to our economy, and who may indeed have been invited to come and live here permanently. Much of the immigration into Britain since the end of the Second World War can be seen in this light. In scale and nature, this immigration has no precedent in our history: it is nonsense to pretend (as some commentators assiduously do) that 800,000 Hindus, or 100,000 Jamaicans or 1,500,000 Muslims, are simply another group of Scots, Irish, French Huguenots or Russian Jews. Furthermore, the lamentable ability of the native population to live too long, its desire to retire from work early, and the disinclination of its women to bear children mean that the future will witness ever larger numbers both of actual new migrants and of British-born ethnic minorities. The population of London is already 30 per cent ethnic minority people, and several of our other cities are moving in that direction. The Office of National Statistics predicts that, of the UK population rise of 7.2 million projected by 2031, 4.1 million will be due to net direct immigration.

It does not do to overstate this: the vast majority (87 per cent) of British people are white and British born – and British bred; 98 per cent of people marry within their own colour/ethnic group. We all speak one language, English. There can by now be almost no one whose *first* language is Welsh or Gaelic, never mind anyone whose *only* language is Welsh or Gaelic. We, the majority, are white; we are born here; we marry someone in the same position; and so we, and our children, belong to the established proprietors of Great Britain –

and of nowhere else. This is as true for the rest of the world as it is for us: 97 per cent of the world's population will live and die in the land in which it was born. As an activity, multiculturalism is a minority lifestyle – with a loud voice.

The post-war arrivals in Britain are people who are here because there is something about our country that attracts them. They make money, and live here more or less peacefully and freely. They derive advantage in being here, and we make money and derive other advantage out of their being here, too. They may also be here because it's fun, for them and us: over and above mere economics, Britain's Hindus, Muslims, Jamaicans, Chinese, East Europeans, etc. now form a visible and cheerfully varied element of our culture. A journey from Newcastle to London makes it obvious that our capital (London) is not what it was 50 years ago, and that it is exotic and exciting in ways in which, I have to say, Newcastle and Wallsend, or Dundee and Kirkcaldy, are not. My children live in areas of London in which I feel myself to be in a minority – as I probably am.

How, then, does (or should) a native like me (a hundred generations of ancestors born here, hideously white, Anglican, Oxford-educated, monolingual and male) relate to these black or brown, Turkish or Bangladeshi-speaking 'ethnic minorities', born in Britain or otherwise? It is not possible for me to deal with this matter from within a multicultural mindset that insists that my nation does not exist – I ignore, for the moment, the argument that it *should not* exist. The evidence for its existence, and for the generally benign nature of its existence, derives, in part, from the evident desire of several millions of people from overseas to come and live here. They clearly know what I know: that this is a good place to live, better for sure than many of the places they come from. In *The Buddha of Suburbia*, Karim Amir's Uncle Anwar, miserable though he was in London, had no desire to return to India: 'India's a rotten place. It's filthy and hot and it's a big pain-in-the-arse to get anything done' (Kureishi, 1990: 64).

The multicultural industry, especially semi-official spokespersons or organisations, is at the moment full of complaints about prejudice, racism, Islamophobia, Hinduphobia, etc. In such an atmosphere, the 'host–guest' paradigm is seen as little more than surface condescension, a form of mannered hypocrisy, now replaced with angrier discourses and more volatile, 'franker' relationships.

I think I may, at this point, permit myself an additional, semi-autobiographical comment. As I mentioned above, I was born in North Wales, where I lived during and just after the war. Life during the war was somewhat restricted, but we often received American food parcels and we were, as the war went on, cheered by the arrival of American soldiers – large, generous, gum-chewing, swaggering young men, who were no doubt a terrible nuisance to everyone but us children, to whom they were great. We (the British) won the war, affirming in that way the moral, as well as the military, superiority of our British way of life. When I was about seven, my father was retrained and sent by the Colonial Office to help run a bit of the Empire, the Crown Colony of Kenya. In this colony, I experienced racism: in one sense, as its beneficiary (whites got most of the best things) and, in another sense, as a kind of victim, experiencing at first hand what it did both to its instigators and its real sufferers, the Africans. At the time, Kenya was preoccupied with the 'Mau Mau'. At school and in the army – a period of compulsory military service for whites – I made it quite clear that I had a problem with using force to retain a territory that obviously wasn't ours. It seemed wrong to be shooting the people whose land it was, in order to retain occupation of it by people whose land it wasn't. This earned me the occasional punch (returned) and, when I left the army, a discussion with a brigadier on the nature of political loyalty and identity. This discussion concluded with an accusatory question: 'Why do you hate the army so much, Davies?' (I didn't hate the army: I disliked the purposes to which it was being put.) When I left for England, our 'house-boy' (a grown, married man) came to see me off. He said that, while he was sorry to see me personally depart, and he was in favour of much of what we *wasungu* (whites) had brought, he wanted me and the rest of us to go, as otherwise his children would be domestic servants, too. This seemed to me at the time to be very fair comment. I hope his optimism was well rewarded.

At Oxford, there was considerable discussion among us 'colonials' as to whether or not we would be well advised to return to countries like Kenya, which were well on the way to independence and where, on even sanguine assumptions, we would be politically and socially marginal. I spent two years studying in America, where, among other things, I went down to Mississippi in the famous 'Freedom Summer'. Mississippi was dreadful, but I considered applying for American citizenship, as I felt at home in the great Republic: it was, to me, part of the story of Great Britain. However, I did return home to England, which, apart from being 'home', seemed by far and away the society most open to whatever talents I possessed. I intended to be academically free and as politically active as I chose; and 'home' was the place where this seemed possible – as it was and is.

I am aware, obviously, that England is not Great Britain or the United Kingdom, and is certainly not Wales; but I will spend little time on such ancient, irrelevant distinctions. I am proud of my country, the United Kingdom of Great Britain and Northern Ireland. I am sufficiently proud of it to be ashamed, very ashamed, of some things in our past – and of much that is wrong now. I am ashamed because, at times, my fellow countrymen have fallen well below the national standards we have. The shame, though, enhances my loyalty; it does not diminish it. When, say, British soldiers are found guilty of abusing prisoners, then the shame, *the humiliation*, that I feel leads not to an attack on the British Army, but to censure of those few soldiers whose behaviour has let down that army – and me. This sense of shame and humiliation is no generalised grief at the sunken state of humanity (though I do tend to subscribe to such a view of the human condition); nor is it grounded in a romantic view of soldierly life. It is a very specific sense of being responsible for – as well as being privileged to belong to – a discrete and onerous culture, expressed best (but not only), and very personally, in the nation into which I was born. I can find in multiculturalism neither a proper sense of being responsible for this nation, nor a commitment to belonging to it. It is as if the claims of multiculturalists to 'be British' are rooted in an angry contempt for, or an antipathy towards, the very collectivity of which they would seek membership. This antipathy takes various forms, occasionally overt and direct, occasionally jolly, occasionally covert and indirect, occasionally acerbic, occasionally vindictive. Overall, it takes the form of a contemptuous ignorance of who we are, and even a denial *that* we are. The next chapter presents the most negative of all the views that multiculturalists seem to hold about us, i.e. that our imperial history makes us indistinguishable from Nazi Germany: we are merely the fascists who won.

CHAPTER 3

WE ARE THE FASCISTS WHO WON: SHOULD
THE BRITISH EXIST?

> Citizenship has been well defined as the right
> ordering of our several loyalties.
>
> (Hadow, 1923: 1)

> All individuals have equal worth irrespective of their
> colour, gender, ethnicity, religion, age or sexual
> orientation.
>
> (Parekh, 2002: xiii)

> If Englishness does not define me, then redefine
> Englishness.
>
> (Andrea Levy, in Stein, 2004: 17)

> An Englishman born and bred, almost.
>
> (Kureishi, 1990: 3)

> But superstition, like belief, must die,
> And what remains when disbelief has gone?
> Grass, weedy pavement, brambles, buttress, sky,
> A shape less recognisable each week,
> A purpose more obscure.
>
> (Philip Larkin, 'Church Going')

All these quotes are about 'identity'. In 'Church Going',
Philip Larkin wonders at his and his countrymen's increasing
diffidence about, and lack of comprehension of, the meaning of the symbols and ornament of the church in which he
found himself. Implicit in the building, its furnishings and its

accoutrements were, as Larkin saw, evidence for the theological, liturgical, architectural, religious and socio-political controversies of the last 400 years – all, as Larkin writes, now controversial to no one, dead and opaque arguments, wrapped in a shroud of incomprehension and indifference. There is now no interest in whatever it was we were once arguing so vigorously about. He is aware, though, that, as he went into the church, he had automatically removed his bicycle clips, in response to some lingering sense of the appropriate.

Into such a world, of 'grass, weedy pavement, brambles', of 'purpose more obscure', of irreverent bicycle clips, come the corrosive certainties of multiculturalism. It has to be said that multiculturalists nowadays have somewhat less confidence in their plausibility, bombs representing a higher certitude; yet it is still the case that multiculturalists (for reasons I do not fully understand) seem to think that the necessary condition for the introduction of their ethnic minority client groups into Larkin's Britain is the vilification and denigration both of what were its values and self-confidence and of what remains of them. This process goes on at a variety of levels, being most freely and graphically employed in the increasing number of 'ethnic minority' works of fiction such as those by Hanif Kureishi, Andrea Levy, Zadie Smith and many others. This subtle and not-so-subtle denigration is particularly strident when the Empire is the subject at hand. It is not so much the question of 'Empire: Good or Bad?' (Answer: Bad), as of the extent to which the Empire *was* the nation and the nation *was* the Empire. And both are portrayed, separately or together, as racist, exploitative, elitist, triumphalist – and in need of expiation and a large amount of punishment. For multiculturalists, the Empire is alive and active:

> The country where I live, among people so unaware
> of our shared past that all they would see if they
> were staring at my aunt would be a black woman
> acting silly. Let those bully boys walk behind me in
> the playground. . . I am the great-grandchild of
> Cecilia Hilton. I am descended from Katherine

whose mother was a slave. I am the cousin of
Africa. . .let them say what they like. Because I am
the bastard child of Empire and I will have my day.

(Levy, in Stein, 2004: 72)

These fictional representations are paralleled in Parekh:

The Rule Britannia mindset, given full-blown
expression at the Last Night of the Proms and until
recently at the start of programming each day on
BBC Radio 4, is a major part of the problem of
Britain. In the same way that it continues to fight
the Second World War. . . Britain seems incapable of
shaking off its imperialist identity. The Brits do
appear to believe that 'Britons never never never
shall be slaves', [but] it is impossible to colonise
three fifths of the world without enslaving oneself.
Our problem has been that Britannia has never
understood itself and has steadfastly refused to see
and understand itself through the prism of our
experience of it, here and in its coloniser mode.

(A 'presentation' to Parekh, 2002: 57)

As many multiculturalists and their client groups have an
origin in ex-imperial territories like Africa, India, Pakistan
and the West Indies, it is perhaps not surprising that the
Empire looms larger in their minds than it does in the consciousness of most of the native white British. Bernard Porter,
in his recent book, *The Absent-Minded Imperialists: Empire,
Society and Culture in Britain,* is quite sure that, while Britain
certainly was an imperial *nation*, she was never an imperial
society. In the minds of most of the British, they were:

A free, moderate and peaceful nation, marked off
from other nations by those qualities, and by the
domestic 'progress' that had formed the main motif
of her history for 400 years. . . The empire, huge
and significant as it was, did not require the
involvement of any large section of British society

for it to live and grow. So long as a minority of men
(and their female helpmeets) were committed
enough to actually ruling it, the rest of the
population could be left to concentrate on other
things. The empire made no great material demands
on most people...and did not need their support or
even interest.

(Porter, 2004: 306–7)

To the vast majority of the British people, the Empire was
somewhere they never went; or, if they did, it tended to be to
the 'ex-colony' America, or to the white Dominions, not to
the actual Colonies or to India: and, of course, very few, very
few indeed, of the native inhabitants of India or Africa ever
came to live here. If the British had stereotypical and hostile
images of foreigners, it was of near-neighbour white foreigners, like the French or Germans or Italians: Frogs, Huns,
Wops – they were definitely nasty, inferior and about to be
taught a lesson. Closer to hand were the domestic 'ethnicities'
of Scots, Welsh, Irish and English, where all could join in the
game of slander and mutual calumny, pouring a mixture of
serious and not-so-serious vilification and sarcasm on each
other.

Porter's view of the cultural 'smallness' of the Empire
does not satisfy multiculturalists. Phyllis Lassner, in *Colonial
Strangers: Women Writing the End of the British Empire*,
says, as we shall see, some very unpleasant things about the
Empire. As it is necessary for the multicultural thesis that the
Empire should loom large in present-day popular culture, she
contrives to describe *the process of losing* it as a 'momentous
...long duré' (Lassner, 2004: 1). She manages to make the
'duré' long by defining the handing over of Hong Kong (1998)
as its terminus. In fact, of course, most of the necessary 'let-
ting go' was done within 20 years of the end of the Second
World War, a period in which most British people had other
things on their minds. The process of 'losing the Empire' was
a major problem or tragedy for a small atypical group of
British people, for whom the vast majority had little sympathy. 'Losing the Empire' was over rather quickly; and Britain

has prospered ever since, the majority neither missing something they never felt they had, nor being traumatised by losing it. Lord Parekh will have none of this:

The end of empire
This is often described as the shedding of a burden whose time has past. However, expunging the traces of an imperial mentality from the national culture, particularly those that involved seeing the white British as a superior race, is a much more difficult task. This mentality penetrated everyday life, popular culture and consciousness. It remains active in projected fantasies and fears about difference, and in racialised stereotypes of otherness. The unstated assumption remains that Britishness and whiteness go together, like roast beef and Yorkshire pudding. There has been no collective working through of this imperial experience. The absence from the national curriculum of a re-written history of Britain as an imperial force, involving dominance in Ireland as well as in Africa, the Caribbean and Asia, is proving from this perspective to be an unmitigated disaster.

(Parekh, 2002: 24–5)

It is to the 'alterities' of the Empire that multiculturalists refer as some kind of 'Ur-proof' of racism in Britain today, ignoring Porter's cautions. Phyllis Lassner, for example, tells an extraordinary tale. She describes her female authors as being heroically bound up in 'British imperial politics', engaged in exploding that 'imperial self-delusion that repressed the violence that would lead to the end of Empire': the Empire's 'ideology of racial supremacy [would] be transformed into a threat not to Britain's global power alone, but to mankind itself' (she is referring to the Holocaust). According to Lassner, authors such as Rumer Godden, Elspeth Huxley and Ethel Mannin

by their collective vulnerability to other imperial antagonists: the Axis of the Japanese Empire and the

Third Reich, from Africa, India, and the Caribbean
to the Middle East, narrated the end of Empire as it
was necessitated by the most horrific and global
consequences of racially defined imperial self-
justification. . . . No matter how we define history,
there is an inextricable relationship between the
'racial modernities' which reached their apogee in
the Holocaust, the necessary and decisive war to end
fascism, the end of Empire, and the indecisive
victories of anticolonial, antiracist narratives. . . The
Holocaust was the horrifically logical consequence
of racist supremacism. . . Hitler's racist policies and
practices represent the quintessential endgame of
colonial oppression.

(Lassner, 2004: 1–16, quoting Burton)

In 2006, an invitation card from the British Empire and
Commonwealth Museum in Bristol invited those interested
to attend an event, 'The Apology Debate: Should Bristol formally apologise for its role in the slave trade?' The card
(coloured very light grey) had on it (in very pale cream) the
following words in this order: Holocaust, War Crimes,
Slavery, Genocide, Dresden, Empire. The British are the fascists who won.

This is a head-on assault on 'who we are'. If we are merely
the fascists who won, then we have little but a malevolent and
sin-laden, self-subverting, self-accusing 'triumph' on which to
base our self-conception as a nation. We do not deserve to
exist. The semi-apocryphal statement 'if Englishness does not
define me, then redefine Englishness' becomes not merely a
legitimately minatory and imperious brusqueness directed
against us, but a life-enhancing, sin-absolving generosity
towards us. We do indeed, in all humility, need to face the fact
that we should (to say the least!) set about 'the decolonization
of the Western imagination [which] means reviewing Western
horizons in the light of collusion with empire and colonialism,
and with the ongoing asymmetries of global power' (Pieterse
and Parekh, 1995: 3). In this task – of removing what we are

and have been (and nearly were – should we perhaps have contrived to lose the war?) – we are offered, as example and
resource, the assistance of the admonitory and, at the same
time, expiatory texts of multiculturalism. It should be noted
that we have to go through this process not simply because a
Britain transformed in the prescribed way would be a Britain
more hospitable to ethnic minorities, but also because *in such
transformation lies our own edification and salvation*. The
British will learn that the official government reports on the
abuses at the Hola Camp at Athi River, Kenya, in the mid-
1950s, failed to spot the fact that Kikuyu women and children
were being gassed there, and at the Ngong Hills camp, in their
hundreds of thousands; or that the British government's dis-
missal of the dreadful General Dyer was a cynical device
designed to camouflage the fact that the 500–1,200 people his
troops gunned down at Amritsar's Jalianwala Bagh in 1919
were merely the beginning of the Final (Indian) Solution, frustrated only by Messrs Gandhi, Jinnah and Nehru. Instead of
fighting them, had we joined hands with our fellow fascists,
the Germans and Japanese, then we could happily have gassed
our way through Europe, Asia and China. What nonsense!
The British Empire may well, in some totally abstract sense,
have been an 'empire' in the same way as that of Hitler and
Hirohito; but, as an Indian reviewer wrote in 1997: 'Had the
Japanese succeeded in penetrating Bengal, the scenario would
very likely have been horrendous, just look at the Japanese
record in Korea, China and the Philippines' (*New Yorker*, 23
June 1997).

Lassner's commentaries, as well as those of her writers,
might sound like nothing more than the irrelevant posturing
of ludicrous fiction. Yet, through the hands of commentators
like Lassner and Parekh, of fiction writers and political pun-
dits alike, this 'imagining' or 'invocation' of 'Empire' moves
from the fantastical and portentous to the solemnly program-
matic. Starting from the fact that we, the British, are merely
the fascists who won, we can benefit from the advice of nov-
elists such as Zadie Smith, who, Phyllis Lassner tells us, says
that, in the very process of migration,

the very idea of empire is being destroyed, so the
identities and positions of colonial and postcolonial
self and Other can no longer remain fixed as
adversarial myths. As they take the risk of
representing and speaking for the colonial Other,
they remind us of those who had no one to listen to
them, they activate a new postcolonial integration.

(Lassner, 2004: 193)

The Empire is gone. What remains is the need to construct a 'new post-colonial integration', heavily freighted (for
the ex-imperialists) with a fascist pedigree that has to be dis-
carded. This new integration must, therefore, take place in
dangerous circumstances – especially for the non-migrant fascist whites: Zadie Smith's 'hero', Samad Iqbal, knows that
'When the walls are falling in, and the sky is dark, and the
ground is rumbling, our actions will define us' (Smith, 2000:
87). Robin Richardson lays out some of the necessary
'actions'. Richardson was the director of the Runnymede
Trust. In his preface to Tariq Modood's book of 1992, he is
concerned to rebut remarks made by Charles Moore in the
Spectator. Moore, according to Richardson, had called for
the exclusion of Urdu-speaking brown Muslims. This, said
Richardson, was 'reminiscent of anti-semitism', and to
counter this racism

it will be vital that entirely different accounts of
history and reality are provided and attended to.
Tariq Modood's account. . .can help us, whatever
our own personal history (whatever that is our own
hyphenated identities) to work with the difficulties
of being British, and of working for a time when
being British is less stressful, and less problematic,
than at present.

(Preface to Modood, 1992: xiii)

To get out of post-imperial stress, Richardson develops a
six-point programme. Among other things, he says, we must

develop 'the concept of hyphenated identity such as Black-British, Muslim-British, Indian-British'. We should realise that 'racial dualism' (categorising everyone as either black or white) is 'an inadequate theoretical framework and an inadequate agenda for practical action'. We (the onus is throughout on the white 'we') must 'realise that religious faith is an integral part of many oppressed people, and is a source of strength for them; it cannot be dismissed as mere delusion or mere so-called fundamentalism'. Furthermore,

> [w]e need to take account of 'the ethnicity paradox';
> the fact that the long road away from racism and
> towards racial equality and justice has often to go
> through spaces where people can know and take
> pride in their own distinctive history, narratives,
> language, tradition.
>
> (ibid.)

And, lest this give the impression that social cohesion might be difficult (especially for the 'British-British'?) while these 'spaces' are being gone through, he concludes:

> We need also, however, to explore and develop the
> concept of commonality – the interests, values,
> symbols, rituals, ceremonies, stories and sentiments
> which large numbers of British people of different
> ethnicities can share and jointly affirm.
>
> (ibid.)

Richardson seems to think that *all* minorities can and should be 'hyphenated' (he has America in mind), i.e. that they are all equally amenable to being led (after a suitable 'space' where they can 'know and take pride' in themselves) to some form of political truce – though he seems to be willing to do without social cohesion while all this is going on. Parekh has a much longer checklist – indeed, the report as a whole is one long list of demands – all rooted in the idea that what Britain was (*if* it was) is no longer acceptable and must change; if not, then 'England, Scotland and Wales are at a turning point in their history. They could become narrow and inward-looking' (Parekh, 2002: xiii).

The turning point

The futures facing Britain may be summarised as static/dynamic; intolerant/cosmopolitan; fearful/ generous; authoritarian/democratic; introspective/ outward looking; punitive/inclusive; myopic/ farsighted. It is the second term in each of these pairings that evokes the kind of Britain proposed in this report. Many customary images of Britain are England-centred – and indeed southern England-centred – and leave many millions of people out of the picture. Increasingly, in Scotland and Wales people have a sense of multiple identity. Englishness is also in the process of being redefined. People in Britain have many differences, but they inhabit the same space and share the same future. All have a role in the collective project of fashioning Britain as an outward looking, generous, inclusive society.

(*ibid.*: xiv)

Not only are we in such a position, but furthermore we can only get out of it by adopting multiculturalism. In Chapter 2, 'Rethinking the National Story', Parekh urges us to stop defending 'old values and ancient hierarchies, relying on a narrow English-dominated backward-looking definition of the nation'. The Commission is sure that 'the movement towards a multi-ethnic, multicultural Britain has been decisive', and that Britain has been affirmed as 'a place where people of different cultural, religious and ethnic backgrounds live together on a permanent basis and strive to build a common life' (*ibid.*: 14).

The Parekh Commission feels that this movement should include schools:

The absence from the national curriculum of a re-written history of Britain as an imperial force, involving dominance in Ireland as well as in Africa, the Caribbean and Asia, is proving from this perspective to be an unmitigated disaster.

(*ibid*.: 25)

The Parekh Report has a long, long list of things that must be done in order to destroy the influence of Empire. Along with schools and the insistence that Britain must declare itself to be a multicultural society (who would do this and how?), it recommends a new Equality Commission, a new Equality Act and a new Human Rights Commission. In addition, we get such details as:

The Legal Services Commission set up under the Access to Justice Act 1999, the Legal Services Consultative Panel, the Community Legal Service and the Criminal Defence Service [should] all operate in ways which guarantee members of all communities fair and equal access to justice.

(*ibid*.: 137)

We recommend that relevant authorities specify the competences and core skills required in relation to race and diversity for all practitioners in the criminal justice system, and ensure that these are systematically considered in initial and continuing training, in recruitment and promotion systems, and in all staff appraisal.

(*ibid*.: 121)

Of course, since the Report was written, the government has set up the Commission for Equality and Human Rights. I will have more to say on this later, and will content myself with noting here that this Commission is recruiting now, and will, in the next few years, be conducting triennial reviews on all public sector bodies to ensure that they are in conformity with the practice of 'equal rights'. From the destruction of the Empire comes an inspector of good racial practice.

There are so many extraordinary things about the kinds of statement I have been presenting above, not least the enormous cheek they exemplify: chutzpah++, perhaps. Any belief we may retain either that we did in some way actually exist, or that, in such existence, we were at least better than Hitler, Mussolini and Hirohito (in whose downfall we played some part), is destroyed by the Lord Parekhs of this world. Trailing a sordid pedigree, we are asked – told, rather – to sanction a Long March by Justice and Equality Commissars through the commanding heights of our highly centralised system of government – all in the interests of several small minorities, of limited importance in our national story. I will not, of course, be allowed to get away with *that* last remark. For, in the present-day climate of expiation and atonement, it is not only the couple of million black or brown people currently resident here that are regarded as fitting recipients of our confession and apology: the countless millions of their brothers and sisters, dead and alive, on whose souls and faces we trampled in our pursuit of Empire should also be the objects of our contrition. We, the not-so-homogeneous non-existing majority, must confess our fascist past and avoid chaos, confusion and perdition by declaring ourselves to be a multicultural nation and expend huge amounts of the energy and resources of our already incompetent governmental apparatus in pursuit of some chimerical equality. Nothing, no fact – for example, that the British Empire was the only empire ever to devote itself to the destruction of slavery; or that we did not gas Kikuyu children, Bengali women or Waziri elders – will suffice to absolve us in the eyes of the Human Rights Hierarchs occupying and operating the compulsory confessional. What we had, what we have, we do not deserve. We took it – all of it – by force and fraud. We are the fascists who won! All must be returned, with interest, to the Commission for Equality and Human Rights. Seldom, since the days of Empire perhaps, can so much have been demanded of so many by so few.

CHAPTER 4

BRITISH(?) GRENADIERS: GATE-CRASHING THE EMPIRE

> There were Africans in Britain before the English
> came here. They were soldiers in the Roman
> imperial army that occupied the southern part of
> our island for three and a half centuries.
>
> (Fryer, in Stein, 2004: 4)

If the sins of Empire are presented as a way of undermining whatever rights the 'majority' might think it has to control the access to the UK of ethnic minorities, paradoxically several of those ethnic minorities fix their title to the British passport firmly to their role in support of, and in having fought for, that self-same (fascist?) Empire. In this chapter I will look at some of the stories of the intertwined military pedigrees of white, black and brown warriors of the Empire. As we shall see, this intertwining creates some confusion about the present-day relationship between the white ('Imperial') majority and the black or brown (ex-Colonial) minorities. Generally, though, we are held to be in debt to these warriors of the Empire. I would like to say here and now that my remarks, where they touch on the exploits of these warriors, reflect a concern solely about their divided loyalties, and imply no doubt whatsoever about their bravery.

This is to be found on the website of the Anglo Sikh Heritage Trail:

> With the end of the Empire, the Anglo-Sikh
> connection did not end. As a legacy Sikhs were
> encouraged to settle in the UK and today they form

a responsible and vibrant part of contemporary
society. . .

Ours is a shared history of courage, sacrifice and
adventure. . .

Cherishing this history brings us. . .to. . .shared
values and aspirations.

(Anglo Sikh Heritage Trail website)

On 19 October 2005, to mark the 200th anniversary of
the Battle of Trafalgar, the *Independent* newspaper had a feature by one Colin Brown. Atop the article was a large headline: 'THE BLACK HEROES OF TRAFALGAR'. It is, of
course, from 21 October 1805 that many of us date the effective independence of this country; and it is on the country's
naval competence that the military foundation of its Empire
rests. From the *Independent* we learned that of HMS
Victory's complement of about 663 men, nine were from the
West Indies and one from Africa. The story went on to say
that 'only' 441 were from England. A closer examination of
the figures showed that there were 151 crew members from
the rest of Great Britain, making the crew just short of being
90 per cent white British. Add the one African to the nine
men from the West Indies (and assume that they were all
black), and about 1.5 per cent of HMS *Victory*'s crew turn
out to have been black. 'Nelson's Navy', commented Brown,
was a 'sea-faring United Nations'. He drew our attention to
an exhibition at Greenwich on 'Black Sailors in Nelson's
Navy'. A BBC programme in the 'Africa Lives on the
BBC' series asserted that 'of the 27 British ships in the battle
[of Trafalgar] many were crewed by black sailors' (BBC,
9 April 2005).

Setting aside the possibility that this is just another
example of the enormous condescension of minorities, even
the average Brit, however crestfallen, chastened, and perhaps
a little chagrined he might be, will realise that a very real truth
is contained in such stories: in the processes of nation-making,
the stories of war and the construction of a military pedigree

are of central importance. As Lord Parekh puts it (as so often, getting it only half-right – I am unaware of the Welsh version of Mafeking):

> Every nation has a dominant national story. . . The dominant national story in England included Agincourt, Trafalgar, Mafeking, the Somme and Dunkirk. There are alternative versions of national history in Scotland and Wales, and in black and Asian communities.
>
> (Parekh, 2002: 16)

The dominant events listed by Parekh are all to do with war. Some years ago I wrote a book, *The Christian Warrior in the Twentieth Century*, in which I looked at war memorials to show how, in their iconography, inscriptions and physical location, they mark out, both literally and metaphorically, the boundaries of 'EuroChristian' Europe, as well as of the separate nations within it. Furthermore, as memorials, they are meant to enable and encourage us to do precisely what the unidentified individual who made the presentation (referred to above) to Lord Parekh seems to want us not to do: they invigorate and re-invigorate our recollection, our revisiting of the meaning of war and of its place in our community and in our history. These memorials, and the rituals carried out at them and at their associated war cemeteries, are to be found all over the world, 'marking out with their dead' (to paraphrase Kipling) the ebb and flow of European empires and nations. These war memorials are the title page of our deed of possession, of what was gained, of what was lost; and in their details and in their telling, and re-telling, we remind ourselves, and we remind the world, firstly that we are not slaves, and secondly precisely *why* it is that we are not.

We are, as has already been noted, chastised by the presenter and by Lord Parekh himself for feeling positive about our story. Lord Parekh and his fellow multiculturalists would seem to find in that story little but more dross from our imperial past.

Most oddly, though, given their obvious distaste for British military prowess, our war-competent pedigree, and our Empire, multiculturalists are surprisingly keen to invest their constituents with the prestige of full participation in such things. As we have already seen, many a multicultural script seeks to confer legitimacy upon the presence in Britain of various ethnic minorities because of their (alleged) direct contribution to the war effort and war-like culture of Great Britain and the British Empire. Ethnic minorities, it seems, had a good war. This is, in the context of the overtly anti-imperialist nature of multiculturalism, somewhat peculiar – indeed rather funny – as the evident incompatibility of being both imperial heroes and anti-imperial freedom fighters stretches the multicultural mythmakers to the limits of their considerable competence.

There are at least two ways of dealing with these apparent inconsistencies. The first is exemplified in the story of the Sikhs and their role in the British Empire in India. Here, as we shall see in some detail below, we find ourselves presented with a pedigree of an initial noble and valorous resistance to the forces of Empire, followed by a 'peace of the brave' made between men (Sikh and British soldiers) now come to respect each other. In this way, *bravery* and *loyalty* are conflated, and hostility *and* loyalty become one; and both parties can share at least some part of the imperial story and subscribe to a common self-conception – a Kiplingesque solution to the problem of East and West. Kipling, it will be remembered, said that this apparently unbridgeable distance between the two would be bridged when 'two strong men stand face to face, tho' they come from the ends of the earth'.

Secondly, there is the simple resort to fable: thus Crescent International tells us about Muslim 'support' for the Kikuyu struggle ('Mau Mau') against the British in Kenya: 'Muslims were. . .among the pioneers of the independence movement. . . The Kikuyu peasants had plenty of support from the Swahili (Muslim) people' (Siddiqui, 1983: 258). This is a novel claim. Muslim hegemony on the East African coast was underwritten by the British Empire, and collapsed when it collapsed.

There is no record of Muslim freedom fighters standing side by side with the Kikuyu in the Aberdare forests of up-country Kenya. The Kikuyu were pretty much on their own, assisted by Muslims no more than, say, by the Maasai. However, such fables keep alive the 'anti-imperialist' credential that is so vital to the *inter*-communal relationships of ethnic minority settlement in Great Britain. The fables are usually more subtle than the one about Mau Mau, and manage to straddle both sides of the story, so that they can help bring about the rapprochement of one minority with another: Sikhs, Muslims and Hindus, for example, played different roles in the story of India's Independence, and were neither then nor now always on peaceful terms with one another. Furthermore, *inside* each ethnic minority there are variations in the 'real' story of resistance to, or cohabitation with, the Empire: the mooted loyalty of old Sikhs to the Empire is not necessarily what young Sikhs want to hear. A diffuse history, a collective multi-layered fable, is therefore necessary to maintain both *inter*-minority and *intra*-minority harmony. This helps to preserve yet another of the foundational myths of multiculturalism, i.e. that all minorities are the same, and all equally benign and at peace with one another and with themselves. Nothing works better for this purpose than stories of joint suffering in the armed struggle and/or joint stories of loyal martial valour, no matter how partial, misleading and mutually incompatible such stories might be.

Within all of this complexity, it is obvious that the main function of these multicultural 'military pedigrees' of ethnic minority involvement in Britain's wars *on Britain's side* is to reinforce the broader purpose of presenting such minorities as being part of our Island and Imperial Story 'for a very long time'. As we noted at the beginning of this chapter, it is alleged that black people were here centuries before the (very white) Angles and Saxons. The 'war stories' of ethnic minorities are part of the project of making ethnic minorities a natural part of the majority. In the strange way of contemporary British multicultural debate, it also has the particular consequence, intended or otherwise, of supporting the propriety of 'quotas' in the British armed forces, an extension to them of the pedigree of the Empire and of the priorities of the Race Relations (Amendment) Act of 2000 and the Equality Act of 2006. It should be noted that, in all of this, the 'British history' (including the military side of it) given us by multiculturalists is a typical example of the house style: a bit of the story is presented as the whole or most of it, and on the basis of 'the bit' is constructed an edifice of putative mutual obligations and shared identities.

The following examples set the military story within the general history of Britain – as seen by multiculturalists. I have paraphrased and abridged them, so they are not direct quotes. The Sikh 'claim' has already been referred to above.

A BBC website assures us that 'Islam has been known in England for a long time: there are references to Islamic scholars in Chaucer's *Canterbury Tales*.'

On 30 October 2005, Channel Four gave us *Great British Islam*, in which a young, female, British-born Muslim television presenter told us that:

- Islam was 'in Britain' 1,200 years ago, as proved by a single gold coin of Offa, King of the Mercians (died c. 796), on which could be found Arabic letters and Muslim sentiments;
- Islam was responsible for the presence in England of horses and formal gardens, coffee and steam baths ('the first alternative medicine in England'), curry ('part of the DNA of Britain'), Bangladeshi restaurants ('chicken masala has replaced fish and chips as the national dish');
- Yemenis in South Shields had 'transformed the social landscape' (not least, one could add, by staging an intra-communal mass brawl in November 2005 – reported in the *Newcastle Journal*, 4 November 2005);
- it was white converts to Islam who founded an orphanage in Liverpool and, in 1889, built a mosque there;

- white converts to Islam sometimes have a hard time
  of it: a present-day young white convert told us of the
  difficulties she had with her family, who did not like
  her conversion to Islam; she also said that we should
  not think that Muslim women were oppressed, as
  they were 'politically on the ball'.

Intercut with this potted history of Britain were references
to our military history. The presenter told us that the Armada
(1588) had been defeated because the Ottoman navy had
helpfully tied down the Spanish navy in the Mediterranean. A
network of mosques, the presenter said, showed the diversity
of British Islam. King George VI, she said, had donated land
in Regents Park for the Central Mosque, in gratitude for the
loyalty of Muslim troops during the Second World War.

At the end of the programme, the young woman indicated
the depth of her patriotism, her joint Muslim–Britishness, by
wrapping the Union Flag around her head as a *hijab*, presumably seeing nothing wrong in such a use of the national
flag.

It is, I suppose, possible to regard all of these contribu-
tions as nothing more than simple helpful and factual presen-
tations of various 'events', and of the contribution to 'Our
Island Story' of various religions and of people of different
colours and nations. They are 'corrections' to our limited,
racist understanding of our own history – an understanding
that masks the debt we owe to our hitherto ignored and unac-
knowledged comrades in arms. Black and brown people, we
are asked to believe, have been here as long as we have, and
are regular contributors to our military successes. If black
men from the Caribbean came in on HMS *Victory*, and not
on the *Empire Windrush*, and were as much responsible for
our (*should* that be 'our'?) victory at Trafalgar in 1805 as the
Ottoman Caliph was for the Spanish defeat in 1588, then why
should anyone regard the presence here, in 2005, of Muslims
and black Caribbeans as anything but normal and beneficial?
Should what was good enough for Offa, Lord Howard of
Effingham, Queen Elizabeth the First and Lord Nelson not be

good enough for us? Are we not all equally the citizen-heirs of one national imperial military pedigree?

THE REGENT'S PARK MOSQUE: MUSLIMS, THE EMPIRE AND WORLD WAR ONE

We have already seen examples of Muslim and Caribbean 'enlistment' in the armed forces of England and the British Empire. The Regent's Park Mosque in London is there because (in one version) a certain Lord Headley, a convert to Islam, suggested to Austen Chamberlain in 1916 that the British government should build a mosque in gratitude for 'the Muslims who died fighting for the Empire' (BBC website, Religion and Ethics section). (Interestingly, Lord Headley's project was partially funded by the Nizam of Hyderabad, originally a Muslim feudatory of the Mughul Empire. As head of a 'Princely State' of the British Empire, the Nizam was a vigorous pro-British opponent of the 1857 'Mutiny'. The Nizam sent his Imperial Service Troop to war against the Muslim Ottoman Empire in Mesopotamia – where it lost 12 men killed in action, four dead of wounds, seven missing and 47 wounded. In the Second World War the Nizam, along with nearly all his fellow princes, placed his soldiers at the disposal of the British Empire. In 1948, Hyderabad, which was threatening to 'defect' to Pakistan, was occupied by the British-trained Indian Army.)

The actual design and construction of the Regent's Park Mosque went very slowly, there apparently being some argument about the appropriateness of the site and about the various proposed designs. It was not until 1944 that the then King George VI opened the Islamic Centre, of which the present mosque is a part. On the Centre's website we are told it was

a gift intended mainly as a tribute to the thousands of Indian Muslim soldiers who died defending the British Empire, which at the time had more Muslim inhabitants than Christian.

This statement, the second phrase rather more enigmatic than the first, may indeed be 'true'. It is equally true that, *pace* Lord Headley, in the First World War many more Muslims died attacking the British Empire than defending it. They were urged to do this in 1914 by Sultan Mehmed V in Istanbul, who associated his declaration of war on the German side, against the British Empire and its allies, with an exhortation to his fellow Muslims to consider

> the very existence of our empire, and of
> 300,000,000 Moslems, whom I have summoned by
> sacred Fetva to a supreme struggle. . .whose faces
> are turned in ecstasy and devotion to the Lord of the
> universe in the mosque and shrine of the Kaabah.
>
> (www.firstworldwar.com website,
> primary documents)

While the 'Muslim empire' did not rise as a man in response to this call from its titular head, the Muslim Ottoman Empire did, of course, join with Germany to fight against the British Empire. The Ottoman Empire lost over 250,000 men in the First World War, many of them killed in battles with the British, whom Muslim Ottoman troops were (often successfully) trying to kill. Amongst British troops, of course, there were Muslim troops of the British Indian Army who were killed and captured, and who died in captivity in Europe and in the campaigns in Mesopotamia, where they perished fighting their Turkish co-religionists. The Arabs, alongside whom 'Lawrence of Arabia' fought, were much more concerned with getting independence from the Ottoman Empire than with supporting the British Empire. At the end of the war they were, of course, bitterly resentful of what they regarded as the treachery of being placed under a British mandate in 1919, and pursued this hostility to the British throughout the interwar period and during the Second World War.

Apart from coping with the Turks, much British effort went into preventing German agents from moving through

Persia to Afghanistan to encourage the king of that country to invade British India. The Germans were hoping that the Afghanis, Waziris, Baluchis and other Muslim tribes would revert to their well-attested hostility to the Raj, and invade British India. While this was no doubt perfectly fair Ottoman–German tactics, neither this nor their activities on other fronts can cast 'Muslims' in the guise of wholehearted defenders of the British Empire. It is perhaps a tricky and rather ghoulish calculation, but it is reasonable to suggest that the main 'Muslim contribution' to the course of the First World War was, Lord Headley notwithstanding, a permanent anxiety about India, the protection by the Ottoman Empire of the South-Eastern Front of the Central Powers, the resulting isolation of Russia, the concomitant prolongation of the war, and generally a very substantial, if incalculable, increase in British and Allied casualties.

Of the entire British Indian Army, which was probably made up of about one third Muslims, 65,000 men lost their lives in the First World War. Of these, then, 20,000 would have been Muslims – approximately one tenth of the death toll of the Ottoman Empire, and just under 2 per cent of that of the British Empire. Many of these British Muslim troops would have been killed by other Muslims. There can be no doubt that there were indeed Muslims in the British armed forces who did indeed fight and die 'for the Empire', and who did so bravely and loyally. It is, however, nonsense to present this contribution from the few as if it represented a general propensity on the part of the world's Muslims to defend the British Empire! Many more Muslims died trying to destroy it.

The end of the First World War seems to have greatly angered Muslims in British India. Hardy writes that 'the mounting evidence of Allied and particularly British intention to smash Turkey enraged nearly all sections of Muslim opinion in India. The victory of 1918 detonated an explosion of Islamic sentiment in India' (Hardy, 1972: 188–90). In July 1921, the All-India Khilafat Conference, agitating on behalf of the Ottoman Caliphate, resolved that it was religiously unlawful for Muslims to serve in the British Army. The Caliphate, of course, in effect destroyed itself by allying with the Central Powers and, along with the German Kaiser and the Austrian Emperor, it went down in their defeat. It was abolished by the Muslim Kemal Ataturk, Turkey's new ruler.

WORLD WAR TWO: WAGING WAR AGAINST HIS MAJESTY THE KING EMPEROR

In 1940–1, the British were in a serious position. They had been expelled from Europe, and the Germans and Italians seemed poised to take over the countries around the Adriatic and the Eastern Mediterranean. Rommel was advancing on Egypt, and the Japanese were destroying the British Empire in the East and were approaching India. A link-up in the Middle-East between Germany and Japan would have made British hopes of victory, survival even, singularly unrealistic. Taking advantage of British weakness and vulnerability, Middle Eastern Muslim leaders, who had long been in touch with the government of Nazi Germany, instigated serious anti-British armed uprisings aimed at driving the British out of the Middle East – and therefore India. Rashid Ali al-Gaylani and Haj Amin al-Hussayni in Iraq, and others in Trans-Jordan, the Lebanon and Syria, were in secret negotiations with the Germans and their allies, and instigated anti-British uprisings of (British-trained) Muslim troops. Egyptian crowds shouted 'Forward, Rommel!' and generally made things difficult for the British Army. Amongst other things, the short-lived regime of el-Gaylani in Iraq organised a *farhud*, a pogrom against Iraqi Jews, before the British Indian Army sent both him and it into exile in Germany. While there, he and al-Hussayni presided over the formation of Muslim units of the Waffen SS, mostly Bosnian Muslims, who fought against the Partisans in Yugoslavia.

These Muslim leaders were, no doubt, motivated by perfectly genuine and popular beliefs, even if they might have been as much misled as encouraged by the Germans: Hitler at some point assured al-Hussayni that 'Germany's *only* remaining objectives [in the Middle East] would be limited to the annihilation of the Jews living under British protection in Arab lands' (my emphasis). (As we shall see, anti-British Sikhs in the 'Indian National Army' were similarly invited by the Japanese to see in them nothing more than the helpful eliminators of the British Empire and the helpful founders of an independent India.) Whether as German dupes, or as patriotic Arab-Muslim leaders, men like al-Hussayni and Rashid Ali al-Gaylani were clear in their objectives: the removal of the British imperial presence in their countries. The two men are clearly authentic Arab-Muslim hero-figures: al-Hussayni lived to become a much-venerated Muslim leader, indeed president of the World Islamic Conference in 1951, while al-Gaylani is well remembered in Iraq. But neither al-Hussayni nor al-Gaylani can, in any way, be seen as heroes of the British Empire ('Who was the Grand Mufti?', n.d.; Hamdi, 1987)!

Muslim Turkey, the biggest Muslim 'player' in World War One, kept neutral throughout World War Two, sensibly watching to see what happened as the war progressed. No doubt all these various tactics made good sense from a Turkish, or Arab-Muslim, point of view; but again, in no way can they be defined as Muslim support for the British, let alone for the Empire. There was no reason at all why Muslim Turkey should support the British Empire.

It was a British Indian Army that overthrew al-Gaylani's regime in Iraq.

In the Second World War, the Indian Army (by 1945 hugely swollen in numbers to 2.5 million volunteers – the world's largest volunteer army) was again about one third Muslim. Some 24,000 men of this British Indian Army died in combat; of these, 8–9,000 would probably have been Muslim.

The British, in an India clearly moving towards independence, had, ever since 1857, been concerned about the loyalty of all its Indian Army troops, not just Muslims. There is some evidence (see Sarila, *The Shadow of the Great Game: The untold story of Indian Partition*) that Indian Muslim support for Britain in World War Two was obtained through the tacit offer of a separate Muslim state – Pakistan, as it became.

LOYAL ALLIES, PROUD BRITONS: THE BRITISH EMPIRE, THE SIKHS – AND OTHERS

Other minorities formed an important part of the British Indian Army. As we have seen, Sikhs (of whom about 400,000 now live in Britain) quite explicitly base their entitlement to live here on what is, indeed, a fairly straightforward steady record of 'on-our-side' involvement in British military prowess and the security of the Empire. At the time of the '1857 Uprising' – in older history books, the Indian Mutiny – Sikh warriors (the *Khalsa*) were called on by the beleaguered British to 'save the Empire. . .they fulfilled their mission'. From then on, Sikhs formed a highly disproportionate part of the army in British India – as 'the pride of the Punjab [they] gave gallant and faithful service' at all times (Grewal, 1990: 136ff).

In the First World War, Sikhs, who constituted just 2 per cent of the population of India, made up 20 per cent of the Indian Army, and fought at Neuve Chapelle, Gallipoli and elsewhere. In the two world wars, Sikhs lost 83,000 men. On its web page 'Sikhs and the British Empire', the Anglo Sikh Heritage Trail (note the title) refers to Sikhs as 'Loyal Allies, Proud Britons', and describes how, amongst other things, they drove back the Japanese in Burma, winning four VCs in the process. Indajit Singh writes on the Heritage Trail that 'Ours is a shared history of courage, sacrifice and adventure. Today the talk is of community cohesion. Cherishing this history brings us closer together to look at shared values and aspirations.' It is worth reminding ourselves of the Sikhs' self-description of the relationship between them and the British Empire:

> With the end of the Empire, the Anglo-Sikh connection did not end. As a legacy Sikhs were encouraged to settle in the UK and today they form a responsible and vibrant part of contemporary society. . . Ours is a shared history of courage, sacrifice and adventure. . . Cherishing this history brings us. . .to. . .shared values and aspirations.

However, the Sikh record is not quite as unblemished as they claim. In the interwar period, the *Babar Akali* movement caused the British considerable concern, especially in the Punjab, the main army recruiting ground. In the Second World War, Sikh troops formed a large part of the men sent by the British to defend the Indian Empire against the Japanese. In 1941–2, the Sikh 'General' Mohan Singh, captured by the Japanese at the fall of Singapore, became the founder-leader of the *Azad Hind Fauj*, the Indian National Army (INA), later led by Subash Chandra Bose. Mohan Singh had responded to Japanese urgings to turn 40,000 or so Indian Army POWs into the INA. He fell out with the Japanese, and was indeed imprisoned by them: Mohan Singh had serious doubts about Japanese intentions, and could not elicit from them a clear commitment to independence for India. He was succeeded as commander of the INA by Subash Chandra Bose, who seems not to have so questioned his new 'allies'. Bose had been busy in Europe, where, under the German aegis, he had helped organise the Indian Legion, made up of British Indian Army soldiers captured in North Africa and Italy. Then, in a kind of re-run of the operation that shipped Lenin back to Russia in 1917, the Germans, hoping to join the Japanese in the destruction of British power in the East, provided a submarine, which took Bose from Berlin to a Japanese submarine, which then took him to Tokyo. From there, he went on to Burma, where he took command of the INA, which accompanied the Japanese in the attempt to invade and occupy Burma and India. Mohan Singh, the original leader of the INA, himself stayed a prisoner of the Japanese throughout the war. His friend and fellow Sikh, G. Dhillon Singh, became the second in command of the 5th, then the 4th Guerrilla Regiment (The 'Nehru') of the INA, and attacked (not very successfully) British positions in Burma (Thompson, 1940; Ramu, 1998).

INDIA'S 'FIRST NATIONAL ARMY'

The Indian Legion and the Indian National Army would appear to have been representative of all of India's ethnic and religious groups: the Indian Legion, for example, had 1,500 Hindus, 500 Sikhs and 500 Muslims. The INA had 17,000 fully armed and (British!) trained soldiers, 25,000 trained men with few weapons, and 200,000 volunteers in waiting. The INA in particular is consistently described in today's independent India as its 'first national army'. The trial of a very small number of the leaders of these units after the war took place to the accompaniment of massive demonstrations in support of the 'mutineers', regarded as heroes of Indian Independence, the founders of India's 'first national army', and a major reason why the British left India. While neither Nehru nor Jinnah had, at the time, openly supported Bose's INA (seemingly taking the view that the Japanese might well have turned out to be both worse than the British and more likely to stay), since Indian Independence the leaders and soldiers of the INA and the Legion have been regarded as authentic Indian heroes. Mohan Singh took his political party, the 'Forward Bloc', into alliance with Nehru's Congress Party, and he became a member of India's Lok Sabha. Dhillon Singh was awarded one of India's highest medals, had a memorial stamp issued to commemorate his deeds, and in 1995, along with 17 other veterans of the INA, marched back along the 6,000-kilometre route taken by the INA to attack the British. In February 2006 he was buried with full military honours. Bose has statues all over India, and is regarded (quite rightly) as one of India's founding heroes. At the sports day of a school I recently visited in Kerala, Bose was the name of one of the 'Houses' in the competition, the other three being Nehru, Gopal Krishna Gokhale (born in 1866, a moderate founder member of the Indian National Congress) and Bhagath Singh, hanged by the British in 1931 for killing a white police officer.

The military 'weight' of the Indian Legion and the INA might have been slight, and of little practical use to either Germans or Japanese. Arab-Muslim uprisings in Iraq and Trans-Jordan may have made little actual difference to the outcome of the war, though it probably did not seem like that at the time. It is not so much what these men actually accomplished – though this is probably more than we think – as how they are now perceived in their respective countries, such as independent India. Indian commentators are insistent, and rightly so, that the very existence of the INA led the British to fear another 'Mutiny', and that this fear drove them to leave India. Certainly, Subash Chandra Bose and the two Sikh generals are seen as authentic heroes of resistance to the British, playing their leading role in the British decision to get out of India. Of Bose's many famous epithets, 'Jai Hind!' ('Victory to India!') is part of India's formal patriotic repertoire. Of their fellow countrymen who, in 1946, led an anti-British mutiny in the Indian Navy – a mutiny backed by a general strike in which 230 people were killed – the *Vijay Times* of India wrote:

> Those patriotic sailors who unfurled the flag of revolt 60 years ago – the upheaval that undoubtedly forced Britain to leave the Indian shores – were a class apart from the present-day run-of-the-mill 'patriots'. As the nation goes through dark hours of faded values and dimmed ideals, let us seek strength from the inspiring lives of those sailors of the RN mutiny because those were the men who sacrificed everything for freedom, our freedom.
>
> (*Vijay Times*, 18 February 2006)

Similarly, al-Hussayni and al-Gaylani are accorded heroic status in their own spheres of activity. This is all perfectly fair. And even though they and the Indian freedom fighters might have found that the Germans and Japanese were not, in fact, easy-going and altruistic, that can in no way diminish the standing of all these men as heroes of the liberation movements of their own people. They cannot, though, be both that *and* members of the pantheon of British heroes, authentic parts of *British* national and imperial history. Nor can a handful of black sailors on board HMS *Victory* on 21 October 1805 make our national independence the fruit of multiculturalism.

THE OTHER EMPIRE

As an aside, we could perhaps consider the contribution to our national and imperial wars of some of our other 'colonies'. In the First World War, 416,000 Australians volunteered, and 45,000 of them died on the Western Front, another 20,000 on other fronts. One million Australian men and women volunteered in the Second World War, of whom 40,000 were killed. Over 100,000 Australians died in the wars of the twentieth century. In the Great War, New Zealand saw more of its citizens killed or wounded per head of population than any other belligerent country. Of the New Zealand population of approximately 1,000,000 in 1914, 100,000 troops and nurses served overseas. Some 42 per cent of New Zealand men of military age served in the New Zealand Expeditionary Force, excluding New Zealand volunteers in other (British) armed forces. Of these volunteers, 41,700 were wounded and 17,000 killed – a 58 per cent casualty rate. While relationships between Britain and the white Dominions have never been easy, and there were arguments and dissenting voices at the time of both wars, there was no flirting or joining up with Germans or Japanese; no inclination to see in Britain's problems an opportunity to humiliate or harm the 'old country'; no laudatory celebrations of those who had sought (for reasons sound enough to themselves) to destroy, not save, the British Empire. Lord Parekh and his contributors might like to consider the following pledge made in one New Zealand school:

> The Great War proved that thousands of our brave NZ
> soldiers thought that this beautiful land of ours was
> worth dying for. We are too young to do as they did,
> but we pledge ourselves, so to live, that when our hour
> of trial shall come, we shall not be found wanting.
> We salute those who gave their lives that we might live
> in peace and security.

Lest this be seen as just another gloss by unregenerate white imperialists, multiculturalists might also care to consider the following. When, on 2 March 2006, the Union Flag was lowered for the last time over the British mission on Nuku'alofa, capital of Tonga, Tonga's prime minister, the Hon. Dr Fred Sevele, said:

> Britain played the most critical and pivotal role in preserving [Tonga's] precious independence and sovereignty. . .which made Tonga the only nation in the whole Pacific to retain her sovereignty. . . To this was also added the extra protection of Tonga's being in Britain's 'Sphere of Influence'. This. . .gave Tonga the soundest of foundations for moving into the modern world with her pride and identity intact . . . And in times of war, Tonga rallied to her ally's [the British Empire's] support. Most significantly, Tongans fought and died for the British Empire in France and Europe, during the First World War. In the Second World War, even more Tongans volunteered, and they fought with valour though with casualties in the Pacific. Despite our meagre resources. . .the people of Tonga bought three Spitfires to help in the war. . . Tonga. . .has remained the faithful friend and ally of Britain's for over 200 years. . . Like the British. . .we Tongans were the warriors, sailors, fishermen, farmers, storytellers, educators, missionaries, and weavers of dreams throughout the Pacific.
>
> (Speech by the Acting Prime Minister, the Hon. Dr Fred V. Sevele, at the formal lowering of the flag at the British High Commission, 2 March 2006, Kingdom of Tonga official website, www.pmo.gov.to/ artman/publish/article_93.shtml, 3 March 2006)

War and the symbols of war are perhaps the most profound and indelible ways of impressing into a culture the boundaries of national and cultural identity. Few nations are constructed on a war-free foundational story. In the case of Britain and many of the ethnic minorities who choose to settle here, the story of war and national identity is inevitably caught up in the complex story of the British Empire. In the various tests of 'citizenship', learning the language, the conventions of voting or queuing, or the proper etiquette at table, are one thing; but involvement or participation in the military culture of Britain and the Empire is another, much more intimate and profound matter. As we have seen, this creates an interesting ambivalence in the world of multiculturalists. They are here, and rightly so, they argue, in part because they fought and died for Britain and her Empire. At the same time, it seems, the British Empire, like all empires, was fascism triumphant. If so, then such a pedigree of minority support is highly – fatally even – compromising to its moral identity. Perhaps, paraphrasing Andrea Levy, it has to be a case of: *If British imperialism does not define me, then redefine imperialism – or me!*

CONCLUSION

Where, and when, does the 'offence of the West' begin? The Crusades seem to have a resonance in 'war matters' and identity formation well beyond their significance. I would guess that few people in Europe could put a date to the Crusades – even after the phenomenon of the *Da Vinci Code*. They are kept alive in strange ways, as in their representation as some equivalent to Islamic fundamentalism today. I have already quoted the comment 'Many assume that religious extremism is a characteristic solely of Islam. The massacre of some 30,000 Jews and Muslims in 1099 by Christian Crusader extremists illustrates that it is not' (West, 2005: 62). It seems odd to me to put an event now over a thousand years old alongside things going on today – the whole sentence is in the present tense; but maybe the author is right. When, in 2005, in Lahore, he offered an 'apology' to Pakistanis and Muslims for the Crusades, the Archbishop of Canterbury, though he was, perhaps, ill-advised to make such a unilateral apology, was recognising how powerful the memory of war – in this case a war that has been over for a thousand years – is to the world's Muslims. Christians may well be rather vague about the Crusades, and may even think that they, now, are not inclined to do the things their predecessors did; and no more are they responsible for such things. The Archbishop, though, was clearly aware of how important these 'bellicognisant' stories are to the self-conception, the identity, of the cultures from which Muslim ethnic minorities come. The current conflicts between the West and some Muslim regimes are often, in Islamic media, referred to as 'Crusader-Zionism'. In Damascus, the huge equestrian statue to Saladin has, around its base, smaller figures of defeated, enchained and cringing Crusader knights, lying next to the bags of booty that they (in this Muslim version) came to steal: war was theft. It is doubtful whether any Syrian or Muslim spiritual (or political) leader would offer, as a gesture of reconciliation, the erasure of such symbols – or, if they did, whether they would long survive as leaders.

It is perhaps the case that such symbols can be (or are) more easily jettisoned or downplayed by societies that are (or seem to be) secure, stable and successful – firmly rooted in their own home ground. It is perhaps the very insecurities of migration, and the comparatively fractured nature of their homelands, which lead Britain's ethnic minorities to adopt various strategies whereby they actually lay claim to being heirs to British military traditions, and participants (however vicariously) in British victories and symbols. It is something of an irony that this roundabout affirmation of a tradition is accompanied by a home-grown tendency, epitomised in the attitude of the Archbishop to Christianity and the Crusades, to make shameful, furtive and negative what had hitherto been regarded as positive and heroic. At one level, Lord Parekh thinks that it is an 'unmitigated disaster' that we have not 'worked through' (he means despise, reject, forget) our imperial history. At another, he (and indeed the Archbishop) might perhaps be thinking where he would be without it. There can be few members of ethnic minorities who would be better off in the lands of their ancestors than they are here.

Perhaps this is why, almost in spite of themselves, multicultural spokesmen and women seem anxious to lay claim, albeit ambivalently, to a part of our military prowess.

At one level this is all rather trivial: did the Ottoman Sultan in 1587 tell Queen Elizabeth that he would help ease the pressure on her navy by sending a fleet of galleys up the Ebro and the Guadalquivir, or did he not? Did more Muslims die trying to kill British soldiers than died defending the British Empire? Is this particular Sikh more loyal today than that other one was yesterday? Yet these apparently arcane questions are not simply of interest solely to historians and armchair strategists. Over and above the role that such military stories play in multicultural pedigree making, which is a serious business, there is the equally serious (and related) matter of the role of such pedigree making in the various efforts to construct the composition of our armed forces on the basis of 'targets' or 'quotas'. If, as seems more than likely, the next few decades will see Western forces involved, in some form or another, in military conflict in lands containing Muslims, or even Sikhs, then how sure can we be of the operational integrity of military units so constructed; or of the integrity of our foreign policy, given the obvious conflicts exemplified, perhaps, in the stories told above? Some comment on this important issue can be found in the later chapter on India, as well as in the chapter on Islam. Before going on to this, I will conclude these four chapters on the Long March through our institutions with a description of multicultural ambitions for our religious institutions – the Church of England in particular.

CHAPTER 5

AN ECCLESIASTICAL HISTORY OF THE ENGLISH
PEOPLE, REVISED

Part Two of the Parekh Report has a concluding chapter on
'Religion and Belief'. On page 242, we read that

> [a] thorough going review of religion in Britain would
> need to consider a wide range of connections, both legal
> and symbolic, between Church and state. Specifically it
> would need to examine the Act of Settlement, which the
> Scottish Parliament has declared to be offensive and
> discriminatory; the Bishoprics Act 1978, which will in
> any case have to be reformed if the recommendations of
> the Royal Commission on the Reform of the House of
> Lords are implemented; the Prisons Act 1952; and the
> Marriage Acts 1949–96, which are widely felt to
> privilege Anglicans over other denominations and faiths;
> customs related to civil religion, for example daily
> prayers at Westminster and various religious ceremonies,
> including memorial events, in local government; the law
> of blasphemy; and the coronation oath.

It is, I have to say, difficult to believe that anyone could
present such a set of 'requirements' in this strangely bland
but presumptuous way. It was at this point that a friend of
mine commented that, faced with such demands, he could
begin to realise how Trotsky must have felt when confronted
by the German terms at Brest-Litovsk. To concede Lord
Parekh's list would indeed, he felt, be 'fleeing from what is
one's own', to quote the then Cardinal Ratzinger's judgement
on multiculturalism.

Her Majesty the Queen was, perhaps, seeking to recover some lost religious ground when, in November 2005, addressing the opening session of the Church of England's General Synod, she asserted the 'unique' power of Christianity to attend to the 'hunger for that which endures and gives meaning' (*Daily Telegraph*, 16 November 2005). Of course, the true significance of this episode lies in the very fact that the *Daily Telegraph* felt obliged to headline it: a headline might well have been justified if Her Majesty had allied herself with a claim for the unique status of Zoroastrianism or Hinduism. It seems remarkably un-newsworthy to report the head of a Christian Church supporting Christianity!

The multicultural impulsion to get us 'fleeing' from what is important about the role of Christianity in the make-up of our collective English identity proceeds along a twin track. There is the attack, as in the Parekh Commission, on the 'privilege' conferred upon the Church of England because of its established status as part of the political and religious system; and, secondly, there is the attack on the role of the Christian religion *per se* because of its 'privileged' position over and above all other religions present in Great Britain.

Multiculturalists, in these purposes if not in all, find allies in the purely secular critics of the role of religion in Britain. The secular aims of Britain's humanists, atheists, agnostics and others would encompass, amongst other things, the removal of the link between the English Church and the English state, although their broader anti-religious aims may well not be acceptable to the many Muslims or Christians. We should, however, preface a discussion of these issues with the reminder that 89 per cent of the population of Britain is classified as white; that over 72 per cent of the population of England and Wales, including many people from minorities, define themselves as 'Christian'; and that all of the minority religions added together amount to about 5.5 per cent of the population. On the other hand, self-defined atheists or 'no religionists' stand at 15 per cent: such agnostics or atheists or 'no religionists' amount to just less than *three times* the entire total of ethnic minority religions. Should Prince Charles wish to be as sensitive to minorities as he would seem to want to be (no matter what his mother might think of this), then he should logically seek to be 'Defender of No-Faith' as well as 'Defender of Faith'.

ESTABLISHMENT: CHURCH, STATE

> A minor national church, that all agree is no more
> than a residue and a token of a historical past.
>
> (Modood, 1992: 86)

This is such a typical example of the arrogant aggressive ignorance of the multiculturalists – and from an author who also inserts Dervla Murphy's saying 'If you know nothing about a people, you can believe anything' (*ibid.*). Who are these 'all' who agree?

The origins of the English ecclesiastical establishment lie in the origins of the modern English state – and *vice versa*. The state was launched into troubled waters, with no guarantee of the survival of state, Church or dynasty. Externally, Catholic powers and the Papacy both threatened and actually carried out armed attacks on England, on the English Crown and on England's allies. Internally, disaffected English Catholics and, increasingly, English 'Calvinists' contended (sometimes violently) for their alternative versions of the government of Church and state. The union of Church and state was, therefore, created in time of war, of threats of war, and of serious internal disturbances, actual and potential. Henry VIII and his successors sought to tie the religious settlement to a newly emphasised national independence, precisely because both of them were vulnerable. Henry VIII's Statute of Appeals declared that

> This realm of England is an Empire. . .governed by one
> supreme head and king. . .unto whom a body politic,
> compact of all sorts and degrees of people, divided in
> terms and by names of spirituality and temporality be
> bounded and owe to bear next to God a natural and

humble obedience; he being also institute. . .with plenary whole and entire power, pre-eminence, authority, prerogative and jurisdiction to render and yield justice and final determination to all manner of folk, residents or subjects within his realm in all causes. . .happening to occur within the limits thereof without restraint or provocation to any foreign princes or potentates of the world. . .

Political and religious life was to exist under the symbolic and legal dominance of the Crown. The English Reformation was, in that sense, a 'lay' accomplishment, mobilised against both foreign and domestic clerical domination, rather than representing or responding to deep-seated spiritual or theological unrest. Thus, from Henry VIII onwards, there was to be no 'special status' for clerics, no ultramontane loyalty, and no independence for religious organisation and religious life. The political cohesion and independence of the realm could in no way be taken for granted. Various Acts of Supremacy and Acts of Uniformity endeavoured to create a single civic religious culture in which all authority was vested in the Crown, at one and the same time head both of state and Church, the secular and the religious foundation of national life. As the seventeenth-century Anglican theologian, Richard Hooker, put it:

There is not any man of the Church of England but the same is also a member of the commonwealth, nor any man a member of the commonwealth which is not also of the Church of England.

(Green and Whiting, 2002: 325)

This was the answer our ancestors gave to the age-old and continuing problem of social order. On the face of it, the Tudor solution might well be seen as having made things worse! Until the Glorious Revolution of 1688, i.e. for well over 100 years from the Henrician legislation, the English (and the other, Celtic, parts of the Crown's dominions) struggled to 'settle' the matters raised by Henry VIII and his dynastic successors. After Henry's Reformation came a Counter-Reformation, persecutions, foreign invasions, a bloody Civil War (in which 10 per cent of the population died), the execution of a monarch, the Restoration of the monarchy, and in 1688 (finally) a foreign-assisted settlement of the basic argument. Only then did Crown and Church seem set firmly in the loyalties of the nation. This was never, though, such 'finished business' as that summation might imply. Neither did the leaders of the Church of England seek to export their model of religious life:

> In these our doings we condemn no other Nations,
> nor prescribe anything but to our own people only:
> For we think it convenient that every Country
> should use such Ceremonies as they shall think best
> to the setting forth of God's honour and glory, and
> to the reducing of the people to a most perfect and
> godly living, without error or superstition.
> *(The Book of Common Prayer)*

For 200 years or so *after* the Glorious Revolution, England struggled with considerable religious (and political) unrest – even though most of the 'all sorts and degrees of people' who had difficulty in living with the new 'constitution' were both English (true-born Englishmen, indeed) and Christian. Catholics and Nonconformists were outside the national system; and there they remained until the second half of the nineteenth century, when formal (if not actual) membership of the body politic was gradually extended to them. English Jews were the other main excluded group. They had been killed and persecuted, and in 1290 evicted from England. Readmitted by Cromwell (on his own authority, and against all advice) in 1656, a mostly foreign Jewish population gradually grew from 400 in 1690 to 50,000 by 1890, by which time (200 years and more after readmission) they were more or less fully integrated into British society. Pogroms in Europe saw further immigration, giving a Jewish population of about 250,000 by 1914.

There have always been, and still are, 'boundary' disputes, both spiritual and geographical, within British political and religious life. The only serious geographical boundary change of the British state in 400 years or so – that associated with Ireland – was, in part, also associated with Roman Catholicism. The semi-separate nature of both politics and language in Scotland and Wales is, in a rather similar way, a function of their distinctive religious traditions. Generally, though, the 'Settlement' of our constitution has given us a stability and longevity without parallel in the world. This is not, and never was, a matter of resting on Henrician or Hanoverian laurels, but rather of an eminently practical political understanding that there is no final once-and-for-all answer to the problem of social order – 'what makes society possible?' It has to be worked on, and worked out, in each generation. Catholics, Dissenters, Jews, Scots, Welsh and Irish – the earlier 'multicultural' elements of Britain – had to wait for many years before becoming an integral part of the traditional systems of British politics and society; even though all of them were, in their own ways, 'founder members' of our religious and political culture. In the city in which I live, the most prominent monument, erected in 1832 and known simply to the great majority of the populace as 'The Monument', carries on its face a rather verbose encomium to Earl Grey, thanking him for carrying through Parliament the Great Reform Bill of 1832, the first in a series of Representation of the People Acts. On the reverse face, another inscription, dated 1932, expresses the gratitude of the people to Earl Grey for helping to make possible what the 1932 re-dedicators termed 'a century of civil peace': 'After a Century of Civil Peace the People Renew Their Gratitude to the Author of the Great Reform Bill.'

Of no other major country in the world could such a term – 'a century of civil peace' – be used to describe the years between 1832 and 1932.

It should be noted that the hundred years here referred to are not years in which, say, a panoply of rights or privileges was conferred on Catholics or Dissenters or Jews *as minorities in a democracy.* There was no democracy. It is very doubtful that Earl Grey, the progenitor of a 'century of civil peace', ever intended that there should be such a thing. Such 'rights' as Dissenters, Catholics and Jews acquired were partial accretions to the obligations and responsibilities they carried as guests in an Anglican society, which had an Anglican monarchy, an established Anglican Church, Anglican universities, and an anglicised, if not Anglican, civil service. The 'rights' they acquired were not privileges conferred on them as a group, but removals of such restrictions as might prevent them from exercising their freedoms and responsibilities *as individuals.* The various Acts of Uniformity were allowed, very slowly, to fall into abeyance, rather than being formally or openly repealed; and in no way did the various acts of 'Emancipation', whether of Jews, Catholics or Dissenters, confer 'democratic rights' upon these citizens. There were, as has been said, no such things – for anyone. The first general election to take place on the basis of full adult suffrage was in 1929, at the end of the period of 'civil peace' referred to on The Monument. Suffrage was the result of, not the precondition for, civic loyalty. The integration of these early minorities proceeded more by incremental accretion, or even by subtle counter-segregations, than by sudden, forced or dramatic integration.

The recently published biography of Cardinal Hume demonstrates very clearly how this process worked. The biography, by Anthony Howard, shows how much England's Catholics lived in a parallel universe. Hume, with a Scottish father and a French Catholic mother, was born in Newcastle upon Tyne, went to a Catholic monastic school, attended a Catholic college at Oxford (carefully avoiding the Anglican theology taught there), a Catholic theological college in Switzerland (language of instruction: Latin!), back to his Catholic school as teacher and later abbot of the associated monastery, then to London as the head of the Roman Catholic Church in England.

Hume's father had met his mother while he was serving with the British Army in France in the First World War. The

Cathedral of St Mary's in Newcastle upon Tyne, outside which now stands a statue of the Cardinal, demonstrates in stone and script how England's Roman Catholics related themselves to the English establishment. It should be remembered that, in the latter part of the nineteenth century, a large Irish immigration radically altered the make-up of England's (and Tyneside's) Catholic population. St Mary's Cathedral was built, so an inscription at St Mary's informs us, with money raised 'by half penny donations from the poorest people on Tyneside'. Another inscription just inside the door tells us of the desires and intentions of those planning the building:

> As Newcastle is alike important for the number of its
> populace, the extent of its Commerce, the greatness of
> its wealth, and the grandeur of its buildings, it behoves
> the Catholic body to erect a large and handsome
> Church, that may be at the same time an honour to their
> religion and an ornament to the Town.

The building, planned in 1838 and designed by Pugin, was finished in 1844. I may perhaps be allowed to point out just how concerned 'the Catholic body' was to be seen to be matching the honour and dignity of the town: they were local patriots – without the vote, without rights, poor.

Another set of inscriptions in the Cathedral tells us that in 1914 'a group of people in the North East' decided to raise a battalion of soldiers (a thousand men or so) from among the Irish Catholics of Tyneside. Four times the required number volunteered, so the one battalion became four, a complete brigade of the Northumberland Fusiliers. Three of these battalions fought on the Somme, where, out of 3,000 men, 500 were killed and 1,500 wounded. Re-formed and re-manned, four battalions fought through the war, winning two VCs, playing a part in the defeat of the German Spring Offensive of 1918, and training newly arrived American troops. The colours of the four battalions were returned to Tyneside: one was laid up at the Catholic Cathedral, one at the Anglican Cathedral, one over the river in Gateshead, and one in the

Guildhall, in Newcastle. In 2001, in a ceremony presided over by Mary McAleese, president of the Irish Republic, the colours of the 27th Battalion were returned to their proper spiritual home in St Mary's. In 2002, Her Majesty the Queen unveiled the statue to Cardinal Basil Hume that now stands outside the cathedral. The initiative for the statue came from the Labour Party, which then controlled the city council. The Labour Party colours on Tyneside were, for many years, green – symbolising its roots in immigrant Irish Catholic political life. The same Labour Party, under the leadership of a Jewish councillor, had some years earlier conferred the Freedom of the City upon Basil Hume – and, at the same time, upon Jackie Milburn, a footballer much admired by the Cardinal. Jackie Milburn is also 'enstatued', but near the football ground – St James' Park.

What is the point of the tale? Just this. The evolving, and never finished, stability of our 'multicultural' society is grounded in nearly 500 years of slow, painfully negotiated compromise, with English and Irish Catholics as with Dissenters and Jews (and indeed others). Nothing was easy in all of this; and neither then nor now were there guarantees of a successful outcome. Yet, at pretty well every stage, these 'minorities' lived, and steadily flourished, within the framework of the Anglican political and religious Establishment. Only one 'bit' of the British Isles, the predominantly Catholic bit, felt obliged to use violence to secede; and even then those fellow religionists of dissident Irish nationalists who were resident in England demonstrated in both wars, as well as between and after the wars, a steadfast loyalty to society, monarch and nation. This loyalty continues. In the 500 years since Henry VIII and his entourage determined that England should be 'an Empire', that empire, for many decades an actual Empire, became a successful and free society, providing an ample home for its religious and other minorities. There might, then, in this story, be some indication that newly arrived minorities should think more of the necessity of learning about and sustaining the set of foundational institutions they encounter here, rather than of trying to dismantle them.

There are some signs that this is understood by at least some ethnic minority leaders – if not all. In 1997, Tariq Modood edited a short book called *Church, State and Religious Minorities,* in which he claimed that, since Prince Charles' 'highly publicised remarks' about wanting to be 'Defender of Faith', 'the question of the implications of recent multi-faith developments [has put] Establishment, the monarchy and the British national identity at the centre of public attention' (Modood, 1997: 3). Whatever the truth of that, to the evident discomfiture of the editor there was little inclination on the part of the majority of the 12 contributors either to back Prince Charles or to support disestablishment of the Church of England. The Roman Catholic Adrian Hastings and Rabbi Sylvia Rothschild were very strongly opposed to disestablishment, while others (Hindu, Buddhist and Sikh) were either gently in favour of, or only very tentatively against establishment. Secular contributors were for disestablishment, as part of their general dislike of religion. The Muslim representative felt that 'dissatisfactions do not by and large relate to the issue of the established church and its privileges' (*ibid.*: 87). The Hindu commented that 'official and unofficial links exist between religion and the government of [this] country. These exist in all countries of the world' (*ibid.*: 75). The Buddhist felt that 'In Britain today we are in the happy position where the state impinges very little on the religious life of its citizens. . .[but] the next King cannot be the Defender of Faith: that job will best be left to trained, effective, secular institutions' (*ibid.*: 72). And the Sikh was quite clear: 'Sikhs are not expecting the host culture and its institutions to make any drastic changes. Contrary to the Sikh's resentment of the majority Hindu hegemony in India, they are more willing to accept the majority community's religious hegemony in Britain. The explanation may lie in their minority immigrant status. . .there should be no resentment of the special relationship [of the Church of England] with the British state' (*ibid.*: 67). Rabbi Rothschild felt that 'to disestablish the Church of England at the beginning of [a] dialogue [about the overall structure of our society] rather than wait to see what would emerge from such a process, seems to me a way only towards mono-dominant and triumphant secularism' (*ibid.*: 60). A Humanist joined forces with an Anglican, feeling that 'Disestablishment would bring liberation for the Churches of England and Scotland and justice to the peoples of these countries' (*ibid.*: 47), while the Anglican – typically – felt that 'the great Reformation principle on which establishment rests, i.e. that the sovereign determined the religion of his or her kingdom, is dead and dreary' (*ibid.*: 38). (Anglicans, or the Anglican Church, should always be ignored. In a plummeting balloon, there would be no need for a first vote on who should be tossed overboard to lighten the load: the Anglican – always earnestly and importunately eager to please – will invariably volunteer.)

In the face of this, Professor Modood (and indeed the later Parekh Commission, to which Modood was the adviser) might well have been expected to drop this part of the multicultural Long March through British religious institutions. But the persistent Professor Modood managed to salvage something from the wreckage – he had, of course, as far back as 1992 dismissed the Church of England as 'no more than a residue'. Having stated at the outset that the issue was 'at the centre of public attention' (an odd claim, it must be said), Professor Modood has (a) to keep the issue open and alive, and (b) to retain the imagery of excluded religious minorities unfairly denied participation in national life. He accomplishes the first in a very strange summation, stating that 'it becomes clear that the situation is pregnant with the unexpected' (*ibid.*: 13). The second purpose, the retention of the imagery of exclusion, is achieved in the sentence of which the 'unexpected pregnancy' is part, thus: 'Once the minorities are allowed [*sic*] to join in a debate previously confined [*sic*] to Christians and constitutional reformers [*sic*], it becomes clear that the situation is pregnant with the unexpected.' There is, of course, no evidence whatsoever that minorities have not been 'allowed' to join in this debate: how and by whom have they not been allowed? Who asked for permission, and from whom? And who refused it? When? Why? What nonsense. In this way, though, the 'exclusion-by-establishment meta-narrative' is kept alive, and the attack on 'hegemony' and 'unfairness' and 'injustice' rolls on. Quite frankly, how a residue becomes pregnant with the unexpected, I do not know.

PLURAL RELIGIONS

One November/December issue of *City Life* (a publication of Newcastle city council), under the sub-heading 'A Special Season for Everyone', had the following:

> Although the Christmas season is important for Christians, who are celebrating the birth of Jesus, many other faiths have celebrations during the winter too.
>
> The popular Hindu festival of Diwali takes place on November 1 this year. It remembers Rama's victorious return to his kingdom when his path was lit by thousands of lights.
>
> The Muslim community will celebrate Eid-ul-Fitr shortly afterwards, on November 3. Eid celebrates the end of Ramadan – a month of fasting. The Hamjoli Group is planning an event to celebrate multi-cultural Newcastle. If you would like to find out more, call the Minority Ethnic Community Support Service on 0191 211 5970.
>
> The Jewish community celebrates Hanukah on December 26. At this festival of light, candles are lit, prayers are said and children are given coins.
>
> Many of our favourite Christmas traditions – such as trees and log fires – come from old pagan customs such as Yule which celebrated the fact that we'd reached the darkest part of winter and spring was on its way.

Throughout our quotidian life, and in such helpful ways, do such casual, amiable corrosions of England's religion occur. The very amiability of such 'invitations' makes them difficult to refuse. How can we object to an apparent equivalence in timing between, say, 'popular' Diwali and 'important' Christmas, even though there is, in fact, nearly eight weeks' difference? Does it matter that the meaning of Christmas is, again in an amiably casual way, glossed with a reference to 'old pagan customs', though no such 'explanation' is offered for Eid or Diwali? Does it matter that the explanation of the date and significance of Christmas (an association with the birth of Jesus) is attached to a dependent clause, which immediately removes any claims to distinctiveness that it might otherwise have?

In so many small ways do we abrade the character of England's religion. There was the attempt by library officials in High Wycombe to ban posters advertising a Christmas carol service because it was exclusive: it promoted one 'religious preference group' (*Daily Telegraph*, 14 December 2003). The same library had hosted a party for a Muslim festival a few days before – this, defined as 'cultural', was held to be different. A similar pusillanimity led Oxfam to refrain from selling Christmas cards, and the managers of crematoria to consider the removal of the crucifix from their buildings. In 2003, the Department for Culture, Media and Sport sent out Christmas cards with Hindu and Muslim symbols, but nothing about Christ or Christianity (*Sunday Telegraph*, 7 December 2003). The Chief Inspector of Prisons criticised prison staff for wearing a St George tie pin, as this could be 'misinterpreted' as racist and had to stop (*Newcastle Journal*, 4 October 2005). As already noted, Prince Charles at some point wished to amend the title 'Defender of the Faith', conferred upon Henry VIII by one of Pope Benedict's predecessors, to become 'Defender of Faith'.

The specificity of history – and history is precisely about specificity – is hidden under various prescriptions and proscriptions. Sir Iqbal Sacranie, secretary of the Muslim Council of Britain, joined with other Muslims to demand the extension of 'Holocaust Day' to cover holocausts in general:

> Holocaust Memorial Day sounds too exclusive to many young Muslims. . . It is a grievance that extremists are able to exploit.
>
> (*Muslim Weekly*, 16 September 2005)

Behind the not uncommon warning-cum-threat, there is, in this particular demand, an evasion of the terrible idiosyncrasy of the Holocaust, the fact of its occurrence in *our* lifetime, on *our* civilised Christian continent. It took *our* armies, and those of *our* Allies, to remove its perpetrators. This is, God help us, *our* Holocaust, which we still struggle to understand. It is no business of Sir Iqbal's, or of his 'extremists'.

Of course, this chipping away at religion is part of the general obsession with political correctness. The Lake District National Park commissars decreed that guided walks should be discontinued because not enough people from minorities were taking part in the rain-soaked rambles. The British Potato Council demanded that the Oxford English Dictionary remove the term 'couch potato', as it demeaned potatoes (*Independent*, 20 June 2005). That same June, the Royal Navy celebrated the 200th anniversary of Trafalgar by having two unnamed fleets (the Red and the Blue) re-enact the battle without mention of England or France (or, one assumes, Spain). French Admiral Mazars felt that French admirals were part of Nelson's Band of Brothers and, maintaining the great French tradition of unconscious humour, he commented that 'the UK Navy [*sic*] and the French Navy are two fingers on the same hand' (*The Times*, 20 June 2005). The madness spills over from the religious into the secular, and back again. It is hard to know whether to laugh or cry, or howl with rage, at such a gibbering of language and meaning. Two fingers, indeed.

The lesson, as the very sensible Sikh and the very sensible Rabbi said above, is to reject demands for the instant deployment of such 'human rights' to which some new minority lays claim, and to insist that change is and should be slow; that movement should be by the minority towards the majority, the majority being long responsible for the steadiness and security of the realm and its moral institutions. The British have had a long – a long and hard – experience of religious multiculturalism and its secular implications. Neither in British Christianity nor in Anglican 'establishment' is there any threat whatsoever to Hindu, Sikh or Muslim, who practise their religions here with a freedom unknown in most parts of the world. These newly arrived religious communities are the beneficiaries of centuries of slow and practical living together, a process of establishing religious 'rights' as being things best left undefined, indeed unarticulated. The vague religious and civil rights of a British citizen are undoubtedly to be preferred to mere human rights:

> It hath been the wisdom of the Church of England, ever since the first compiling of her publick Liturgy, to keep the mean between the two extremes, of too much stiffness in refusing, and of too much easiness in admitting any variation from it. For, as on the one side common experience sheweth, that where a change hath been made of things advisedly established (no evident necessity so requiring) sundry inconveniences have thereupon ensued; and those many times more and greater than the evils, that were intended to be remedied by such change: so on the other side, the particular Forms of Divine worship, and the Rites and Ceremonies appointed to be used therein, being things in their own nature indifferent, and alterable, and so acknowledged; it is but reasonable, that upon weighty and important considerations, according to the various exigency of times and occasions, such changes and alterations should be made therein, as to those that are in place of Authority should from time to time seem either necessary or expedient.

The Preface to the *Book of Common Prayer* should be read by all members of minority religions who wish to understand the religious and civil basis of the country in which they have the luck and privilege to live. The natives should read it, too.

CHAPTER 6

FALSE COMPARISONS

Minority ethnic communities. . .[are] residentially
clustered in urban conurbations. 70% of minority
ethnic communities live in the 88 most deprived
areas. Some ethnic groups experience much higher
unemployment and lower pay than the population at
large.

(White Paper *Fairness for All: A New Commission
for Equality and Human Rights*, 2004)

The ethnic minority population is growing fast, is
getting richer, and, in some groups, is educated to a
higher level than the general population. Trends also
indicate that the economic position of ethnic
minority groups in Britain will improve significantly
over the next decade.

(ETHNOS: Research and Consultancy website, 2006)

Patterns of mortality and morbidity are more serious
in Asian, black and Irish communities than in the
population as a whole.

(Parekh, 2002: xix)

They [new Commonwealth immigrants] experience
both advantage and disadvantage in British society –
some of these groups have incomes above the
national average.

(Modood, 2005: 3)

The relatively 'optimistic' tone of two of these quotes indicates that attitudes are changing in multicultural gatherings, and that a little reality is creeping in: I refer, in particular, to Lucinda Platt's excellent 2005 article 'Migration and Social Mobility'. The dominant discourse, though, still casts ethnic minorities in the role of 'lowly victim': thus, for example, the *Muslim Weekly* of 22 December 2006 headlines 'Islamophobia Plagues Europe.' What nonsense. It is necessary to assert two things very firmly:

1. In all four quotes at the beginning of this chapter, the standard of living of (black or brown) ethnic minorities is established by reference to the (white) majority: the white majority is presented as the proper comparator. This seems nonsense to me. Migrants come to Great Britain because life *here* is better than life *there* – whether 'there' is: Pakistan, Bangladesh, Orissa, Jamaica or Somalia. The proper comparator is how they are here with how they were there, and how they would have been had they stayed there. There can be few members of any ethnic minority who would be better off in the land they and/or their forefathers came from.

2. Given the demographic nature of migration, it would be a statistical miracle for the distribution of ethnic minorities, on any variable, to match that of the native ('white non-migrant') population.

There can be few members of any ethnic minority currently resident here in which the latest generation is both worse off than where they originated and worse off than the original migrants. The latter are a second proper comparator. Such socio-economic measures are, of course, only part of the story, saying nothing about, for example, levels of governmental corruption, systematic and officially condoned police and military violence, or degraded public health systems – all of which are more likely to be found 'there' than 'here'.

It seems important to me that these simple truths are firmly registered. Otherwise, all we will ever see in the multiculturalist view of migration to the UK is a stream of endless groups of people endlessly seeking an injustice in which to settle. Having said that, what can we make of the presentation to us of the cast-down misery of ethnic minorities? Take, for example, this headline in the *Muslim Weekly* of 26 August 2005: '60% Muslims Live in Abject Poverty'.

Or the following frequently heard pronouncement, this particular version originating from the Commission for Racial Equality (CRE): 'There are more black men in British prisons than there are in British universities.'

'Devastating', said the chairman of the CRE. But what do such statements mean? That the hundreds of thousands of Indians, Bangladeshis and Pakistanis who voluntarily migrate, or migrated, to the UK, often with great difficulty and at great cost, and expressly to earn (and remit) money, are fundamentally mistaken and stupid? That they should realise their mistakes and go home, to a poverty that is presumably at least somewhat less 'abject' than the poverty they endure here? Does the comment about black men, prison and university mean that, in order to engender a degraded and imprisoned life for black British men, the non-migrant white 'host' community has deliberately constructed and administered, in a publicly visible, totally illegal way, an extraordinary collusion between the entire judicial system and the admissions policies of over a hundred British universities?

There is obviously, somewhere, a reality or truth about the lives in England of black people, Muslims, brown people, Hindus, Zoroastrians, etc. To wrap this reality around with such comments produces an image that is as allusive and misleading, as fictive, as you can get. They tell you much about the speaker and little enough about the alleged subject. It might be objected that the two examples given above are not so much 'raw data' as interpretations made of them. Perhaps. But the interpretation made of them is designed, in both these instances, to imply malevolent intent ('institutional racism') on the part of the indigenous or 'host' society, and to cast various minorities as being – yet again – passive, manipulated victims of that malevolence. White people are presented as nasty and cunning; black people as weak and pathetic. Such malevolence imputed to the whites and such feeble stupidity imputed to the blacks form one of the basic meta-narratives surrounding the lives and experiences of ethnic minorities – as articulated by the multicultural Establishment.

PAKISTAN – A GOOD PLACE TO LEAVE?

The *Muslim Weekly* headline elides or camouflages the realities of the experiences and behaviour of Pakistanis in Britain. The 'abject poverty' of UK-dwelling Pakistanis is a figure derived from the General Household Survey, which 'defines poverty' as 60 per cent or less of the British national median income. Such an income is several orders of magnitude above the national median income of Pakistan – surely one, if not the only, serious comparator. The relatively low skill level of many Pakistanis, and the associated low pay – a factor picked out by the General Household Survey – goes unmentioned by the *Muslim Weekly*. In Pakistan itself there is a labour force participation rate of 30 per cent. Thirty per cent of those actually at work do 56 or more hours per week, prompting the Pakistani Federal Bureau of Statistics to comment on the 'prevalence of less than subsistence wages in the job market' (Government of Pakistan, *Labour Force Survey 2001–2002*). The Pakistani Labour Force Survey collects, as a matter of routine, data on the occupational health of all employees *over the age of 10,* a datum not available for Bradford or Tower Hamlets, where child labour is both illegal and unknown. Data on the importing of brides from Pakistan and Bangladesh show that, for example, it is very likely that Asian children born in Tower Hamlets or Bradford will have a foreign, non-English speaking mother and a concomitant disadvantage in school. Fifty-five per cent of all births in Inner London are to foreign-born women (Immigration Watch website, 2006). The overall female literacy rate in Pakistan is 37 per cent, less in the rural areas.

The *Sunday Telegraph* of 23 April 2006 said that the people of the Indian diaspora are estimated to be worth, globally, $350 billion dollars. Special banking arrangements, advertising on websites and elsewhere, facilitate the transmission of substantial amounts of this wealth back to India.

Clearly, Indians are not Pakistanis; but Roger Ballard and others have documented the process of remitting money between Pakistan, Great Britain and the Middle East (Ballard, 1987). In spite of their 'abject poverty', Britain's Pakistanis are able to remit to their homeland many millions of pounds each year, part of the £2.7 billion that is annually remitted from the UK (*The Times*, 17 November 2005). Migration has been an enormous boon for Pakistani and other migrants.

Such considerations are seldom mentioned, clashing as they do with the basic meta-narrative, which has to see ethnic minorities as in some way unjustly treated because they are not as well off as the native whites.

BLACK BRITISH STYLE

The Commission for Racial Equality, particularly fond of the 'black/prison/university' slogan, is also in the business of spinning a story of the unfairness of it all. When I asked Mr Nick Johnson of the CRE for a comment, he replied: 'the statistic is taken from widely available data [and] I made the point to illustrate that there is still large-scale inequality of opportunity in this country' (private communication, November 2005).

The 'statistic' does nothing of the sort. Indeed, the CRE's own 'statistic', given to the Parekh Report, shows that, of first-year students at British universities, African and African-Caribbeans are represented at over twice their incidence in the population as a whole (Parekh, 2002: 377): Africans account for 0.4 per cent of Great Britain's population of 18–24-year-olds, but they produce 2.2 per cent of the university population, while the respective figures for Afro-Caribbeans are 0.9 per cent and 2 per cent. There may well be twice as many black men in British prisons as there are in British universities. There are also twice as many black women in British universities as there are black men in British universities. The Parekh Report ignores its own facts and tiptoes past its own figures with little comment – figures that show, amongst other things, that the only group to be under-represented at university is the white group (*ibid.*).

The CRE is hugely disinclined to address the idea that the relatively high crime rates among young black men, and their relatively indifferent performance at school, render unsurprising the profile of their statistical distribution in prison and university. When David Lammy, the 'black parliamentary undersecretary at the Department for Constitutional Affairs' (*Daily Telegraph*, 15 December 2003), tried to explain the figures by saying 'it's an unspoken truth that few black youngsters aspire to go to university, it's a phrase hardly mentioned to them when growing up', he managed to mask the difference between young black men and young black women – the latter seem to have heard the word 'university' quite frequently. Young black men are the problem: they seem to live in a different world.

Gun crime, hard drugs and indifference to marriage (promiscuity, in a word) were, and remain, a characteristic of Jamaica, where many of Britain's black men and women come from. In Jamaica (population 2.7 million) itself, in 2005 there were 1,500 murders, an increase of 13 per cent on the year before; 125 people are killed there every month; 77 per cent of these killings are by gun. The Jamaican police, in 323 violent confrontations, killed a further 141 people, up by 52 per cent on the previous year. (Meanwhile, the British police are dragged over the coals because of one, most unfortunate and tragic, accidental killing of an innocent but illegal immigrant.) Three schools had to close in Jamaica in 2005 because of guns either in the school or in the vicinity. Jamaica is a major entrepôt for the drugs trade and the associated trafficking of arms and ammunition. Politics and gangs inter-relate, producing extensive corruption and what the prime minister called 'the country's slow descent into anarchy'. Jamaica's economy is being wrecked by crime. Jamaica's National Security Plan (NSP) for 2005 (which is *not* concerned with national defence against an outside enemy) states that 'Jamaica has spawned a culture of violence in its most negative form, which is abhorrent to its values, and stands in the way of every kind of social progress' (National Security Plan, Government of Jamaica website, and websites of the *Jamaica Gleaner* and the *Jamaican Observer*). It scarcely needs to be said that most of this mayhem is a male lifestyle.

It might be thought that what is going on in Jamaica is of only marginal relevance to young Jamaican men living in Britain, many or most of whom are British born. Given modern travel facilities, this, of course, in no way precludes connections with Jamaica itself. Mr Darcus Howe, a 'black activist', describes a conversation with a couple of 'Yardies' (Jamaican criminals), who bragged that a hitman could 'commit an execution' (*sic*) one day, get on a plane to Jamaica, and return to England the following day with a new name, passport, NI number and so on: these gentlemen regarded Jamaicans resident in Britain as 'idiots' (*New Statesman*, 3 March 2003). Graeme McLagan (*Guns and Gangs: Inside Black Gun Crime*) provides a sobering account of the extent to which what is going on in Jamaica seems to be being replicated in England and reinforced or underwritten by ease of contact between the two places. *British-born* black men were responsible for 80 per cent of the 'black on black' murders covered by the police's 'Trident' operation in London; Jamaicans were responsible for 18 per cent of these (McLagan, 2005: 151). At Heathrow, 76 per cent of non-UK nationals caught with drugs in 2001 were Jamaican, part of the major drug-importing business centring on Jamaica (*ibid.*: 121). Of the 10,000 *non-British nationals* in British prisons, over 2,000 are Jamaican. One female inmate in five is a foreign national, and most of these are Jamaicans, jailed for drug smuggling. It would appear that there are, as McLagan and other writers show, differences in the crime styles of Jamaican-born Jamaicans and their British-born fellows; but not necessarily in the direction of greater observance of the law. This may be unduly pessimistic: Mr Darcus Howe, quoted above, gave the views of some British-born Jamaicans on their drug-ferrying brothers and sisters: 'sen back dey rass', which apparently translates as 'deport the bastards' (*New Statesman*, 3 March 2003). This seems quite a reasonable attitude to me.

It is now, of course, difficult to get accurate figures on the criminal (or law-abiding) behaviour of black men, or men by origin coming from the Caribbean: the very collection of such data is held to be 'politically incorrect'. Even so steadfast a reporter as Norman Dennis, whose analysis of the Macpherson Report (Dennis, 2000) broke new ground in demonstrating the corrosive power of racialised (i.e. skewed) crime reporting and judicial inquiries, cannot bring himself to comment too explicitly on this matter. In *Cultures and Crimes, Policing in Four Nations,* Dennis provides ample (and scary) proof-data on the geometrically increasing crime rates of post-war Britain, the vast bulk of it, of course (like our general decadence), home-grown. Amidst a welter of hard fact, Norman Dennis provides the following data on crime in the London Borough of Lambeth, where 34 per cent of the population is from ethnic minorities. 'Black Caribbeans' make up 12 per cent of the population of Lambeth – the highest proportion in London. In 2001, from February to December, there were never as few as 400 recorded robberies *a month* in Lambeth. Dennis contrasts this figure with that for England and Wales, from 1893 to 1941, when there were never *as many* as 400 recorded robberies *a year*! As late as 1997, the total number of robberies was never higher than 12,891. In 2002/3 there were 108,000 robberies in England and Wales. Between 1999 and 2003 there were 18,600 police-recorded robberies in Lambeth alone, of which 1,300, or 7 per cent, were cleared up (Dennis, 2005: 56ff).

So in Lambeth there is a lot of crime, and the criminals have little fear that they will get caught, i.e. that victims and witnesses will feel able to stand up in court against them. Again, McLagan provides ample evidence of the power of black criminals in their 'communities', where intimidation and informal 'patterns of control' give the police a very hard time indeed. In 2001, 3,000 police and 300 civilian assistants were mobilised in connection with the Notting Hill Carnival. Two men were murdered, and the police made over 400 arrests. Officers were particularly concerned with the rapidly rising level of crime associated with the illegal importation of cocaine from Jamaica.

I am, of course, open to the comment that crime *in* a community is not the same as crime *by* a community. Fair point.

But it is also a fair point that it beggars belief to think that all this crime taking place in Lambeth is carried out by criminals coming into Lambeth from, say, Bootle, County Durham, Carlisle or Inverness. It is certainly the case that black citizens are twice as likely to be concerned about crime in their neighbourhood as are whites: 37 per cent of blacks, 18 per cent of whites (*ibid*.: 63). This mirrors the Jamaican NSP finding that 55 per cent of Jamaicans give crime as their main concern – not surprising when the detection rate for murder (the most 'obvious' of crimes) is 40 per cent and falling, and where police killings, perhaps in response, are rising very rapidly.

As noted above, when I asked Mr Nick Johnson of the CRE for a comment on his use of the 'more-black-men-in-prison-than-at-university' mantra, all I received was a repetition of the line that we live in an unequal society. Mr Johnson is not alone in believing that the world of ethnic minorities is a world devoid of justice. It is full of hate and racism flowing one way. 'The reality is social deprivation, racism and Islamophobia, [the] obstacles to Muslims being a full part of British society' (*Muslim Weekly*, 26 August 2005). 'I've felt persecuted from day one by everyone who isn't black', says Darcus Howe (*The Times*, 20 October 2005). When such posturing is coupled with the reality-ignoring attitude of the Parekh Report – that the changes necessary within black and Asian communities 'are best identified and undertaken *by each community separately*' (Parekh, 2002: x, my emphasis) – then no conversation can exist beyond the articulation of grievance and the blaming of someone, or something, else. In such ways, the broader picture – of both the majority and the several minorities – is made invisible by the tactics adopted by these special pleaders. As the various ethnic minorities equip themselves with representative organisations and spokespeople, and with the vocabulary of multiculturalism, then we have little more than the prospect of a world of endless complaint.

Oddly, perhaps, the very early stories of migration and diaspora were more at home with a morality play, contrasting the life in the original 'home' (i.e. somewhere other than the

UK) with the experience of living or settling in London or elsewhere in Britain. These stories were, of course, often enough characterised by nostalgia, grumbles about the weather, concern about racism large and small. But often enough, too, there was an awareness that England offered certain advantages not available in, say, Bangladesh or Jamaica. To that extent they were aimed at convincing those 'at home' that there was some benefit in migration. The comparator, then, was the reality of the immediate contemporary life in (say) Bangladesh, which was contrasted with the day-to-day experience of life in England. Such comparisons may have included comment on the life in Bangladesh of parents or grandparents – the kind of comparison that is, of course, made by many native-born British people ('non-migrant whites') like me, to whom the last two or three generations have been remarkably benign.

A PROPER COMPARATOR

The multicultural world will have none of this. Oddly, while insisting on the reality of a multicultural *world*, they insist on the propriety of a comparator of one country *only* – the UK. Institute upon multicultural institute will either engage in research or delve into official British figures (rather like Karl Marx in the British Library) and, deriving injustice from the norms or statistical distributions covering the general (i.e. mainly native-born and white) populations, create all sorts of evident 'injustices'. I have already instanced two of these – the prison/university nostrum peddled by the CRE, and the headline in the *Muslim Weekly* that had Pakistanis in Britain living in 'abject poverty' – and this in the same month as earthquakes further reduced into seriously abject poverty the already abjectly poor of Pakistan, surely (along with Jamaica) one of the least admirable countries in the world, and one of many in which, quite frankly, you are best advised not to live. Neither the CRE nor the *Muslim Weekly* is alone in propagating the silly view that the presentation of a statistic showing that a particular ethnic minority is, say, less wealthy, or more ill, or doing worse at school than the white or native

majority, or than some other minority, is on its own a sufficiently powerful case for moral outrage at the state of *our*
nation! This is not a question of mere definitions and techni-
calities, such as the familiar arguments about the meaning of
the term 'poverty' or the definition of 'health', or the determi-
nants of 'educational progress' in our school system. It is the
very fundamental question, when dealing with ethnic minorities: *to what do they compare themselves?* It seems hugely
obvious to me that the proper comparator, or (as a compromise) *one* proper comparator, is the society or country from
which they come: and it is hard to think of many such societies or countries that are as generous as England in the
provision of a decent style of life and a decent standard of
living. Is everyone here equal? No. So?

I am aware that an increasing number of members of
ethnic minorities are born here: they are 'British born', and
therefore (so the argument runs) the proper comparator is
indeed the average or normal distribution of goods, services
and opportunities in the UK, now.

I have to say that I find it almost impossible to regard,
say, a Jamaican or Pakistani born in the UK, even second generation, as being 'British' in the same way as I am British. As
far as I know, every single one of my ancestors, through generations that stretch into the mists of time, was born, lived
and died here, in Great Britain. But even granting my common citizenship with people from Jamaica, Pakistan, Poland,
Bangladesh, if common citizenship is what we have, why
should not the *grandparents* of a Bangladeshi or Punjabi,
perhaps living all their lives in and never leaving their place
of birth, be seen as the benchmark by which to evaluate
the British experience of their British (i.e. born in Britain)
grandchildren? I can think of few grandparents or great-
grandparents, looking down perhaps, or across the conti-
nents, who could possibly be persuaded to see the lives of
their progeny as being anything other than a material
improvement on their own. *As children*, one of my grandfathers worked down a coal mine and the other was on
coastal sailing ships. My maternal grandfather had to run

away from home because *his* father, my great-grandfather, was a violent drunk, who ended up in the workhouse mental asylum. My paternal grandfather had to go down the mines to work because his parents needed his wages to feed their other children. May God smile upon them both. *They are my comparator*, the measure of how far my life (in a material sense anyway) has improved over two generations; as, indeed, has the life of my children. The same comparator is available to any ethnic minority member, British born or not. In making such a comparison, and in setting aside others, they, like me, would be better advised as to the nature of their little bit of the human condition. There can be very few members of ethnic minorities who would be better off back in their ancestral lands.

BLACK BRITISH STYLE: STRING VESTS TO SUNDERLAND, MAY 2006

Sometimes these matters descend into farce – especially when Britain's cultural establishments get involved in the business of promoting 'difference' – as, no doubt, various governmental policies invite them to do. Indeed, in the *Daily Telegraph* of 12 May 2006 we read that the director of the Art Fund had complained that the government policy of 'improving access, social inclusion, out-reach and education' was depriving museums of cash to buy important works of art. The deprived regions, such as the North East, are the beneficiaries of such a policy of 'social inclusion'. As something of a light-hearted comment on the fundamental silliness of this policy, I offer you the following account of a visit a friend and I made to an exhibition sent to Sunderland by the Victoria and Albert Museum.

At Sunderland's Museum and Winter Gardens in 2006, Mackems and Geordies* were able to view a string vest sent up by the Victoria and Albert Museum as proof of loyalty to Prince Albert's desire that culture should have an outing in the

---

* Mackems are people unlucky enough to live in Sunderland; Geordies are those blessed people who live in Newcastle.

less cosmopolitan regions of His Wife's kingdom. The string vest was part of 'Black British Style', presented by the Tyne and Wear museums service (of which I was once chairman), and entry was free. A helpful large-print notice (ENGLAND IS THE PLACE FOR ME) told us that 'Black style has dramatically reshaped the visual landscape of Britain. . . The black British body can devise its own distinct visual identity and can continually say something about the place of black people in Britain.' This was true.

Another large-print notice (CALLING RASTAFARA HALLELUJAH!) and a continuous video presentation depicted a group of young black men wearing large hats and dancing around. These were, if we understood things correctly, 'Rastas', and their garments and behaviour expressed an 'anti-colonial stance', enabling them to 're-claim their African heritage in the face of the hostile opposition they experienced in Britain'. Another continuous video showed the earliest black men disembarking from a ship (probably built on the Wear), wearing conventional double-breasted suits and seemingly off to look for work: 'The question of one's place became more contested than anyone had ever imagined', said another notice. A photo flanked by yet another large-print notice (ORIGINAL PINKY DANCE HALL QUEEN 1989–2003) showed us 'Original Pinky' in relaxed mode. Original Pinky 'wore' a dress that at least kept her ears warm: the notice told us that she was a model of 'salacious lyrics and sexually overt dance styles. . .sexually provocative: but it is seen by Professor Carolyn Cooper as a source of empowerment in the wearer'.

Near the string vest, another notice (FIX UP LOOK SHARP) told us that 'Black dress and black music have come to define eras, signal seasons of moral panic. . .the body-conscious "barely-there" style of dance hall is matched with the salacious sounds of. . .the smooth rhythms of Lover's Rock echoed in the man's camel coat.' There was a photo of a man in a camel coat. WIN THE LOST AT ANY COST and NATION OF ISLAM HYDE PARK LONDON 1993 introduced us to black religion. By now on the lookout for a little less salaciousness, we approached. The black Church was, we were told, something that 'has been termed "a system of meaning" to explain who believers are and the world they live in'. White churchgoers had rejected black churchgoers; but 'how the body is dressed must reflect the wearer's morality and spiritual devotion', marking them out from non-believers; but dress codes are now more relaxed and 'it is no longer compulsory to wear a hat to service. Make-up can now be worn, as can jewellery and trousers: the reverence black churchgoers pay to their respective beliefs is never at the expense of their sense of style.' Men, too. Various photos demonstrated the truth of this observation. The Nation of Islam section looked a bit sombre: but another large-print notice drew our attention to the fact that, even though females of that faith are under some pressure to be modest, 'as the photo shows, modesty can be upheld, while engaging with glamour'. This referred to a photo of a Nation of Islam matron jumping up and down, engaging very nicely with glamour. RESPECT YOURSELF surmised that 'culture and style [are] a symbolic aspect of our resistance, our determination to be different from others, to have something we can say that is our own. . .they sought alternative dress styles. . .and hair styles such as the afro, the dashiki, the afro comb and the leather "shaft" coat, key components of what Dr K van Dyke Lewis calls the "archive of black style", one which reaffirms black resistance and black identity'. The string vest was near the door as we went out, next to a tableau entitled CAMOU-FLAGE JACKET CAMOUFLAGE TROUSERS BASEBALL CAP T-SHIRT BUCKLE BELT ARMY BOOTS. This referred us to a rap group called Public Enemy and their album *Yo! Bum Rush the Show*, in which they appeared dressed in army uniforms, carrying Uzi guns: 'the look became popular as an expression of black consciousness'. In T-SHIRT a modern rifle-sight picked out a target on the T-shirt wearer's chest.

We learned later that the funding agreement signed between the Victoria and Albert Museum and the DCMS (Department for Culture, Media and Sport) includes, as a 'key goal', an increase of a third in the number of children visiting museums, art galleries, etc., thereby promoting 'excellence'. The second strategic purpose sets the V&A in the direction of delivering 'projects that are sustainable and engage under-represented audiences'. It is no doubt true that few people in Sunderland would have been able, without such support, to see this exhibition of 'Black British Style'. We rather felt, though, that a comment to the Commission for Racial Equality would have been in order, since the depiction of Black British Style, with the exception of those steady-looking men coming off the ship, makes black Britons out to be a bunch of sex-obsessed layabouts who wear string vests. Is this fair? Is it a good model for our young? Does anybody care? As it happens, downstairs in the Sunderland Winter Garden was a display devoted to another group of 'black' men, miners, now all gone.

Is this really how black Caribbean people wish to be seen? Are we, the white citizens of Sunderland and Newcastle, actually meant to take this seriously? If so, what is it that we are being asked to take seriously – a caricature, a cartoon? Are 'we', in comparing ourselves to 'them', meant to see us, or them, as the exemplar?

MADE IN BRITAIN

The ideological implications of the choice of comparator are extensive, and permeate much of this book. This chapter concludes by noting that the 'comparator issue' is implied in the form of national 'conversation' about multiculturalism that goes like this:

> *Native, non-migrant white Briton*: If you don't like it, go home!
> *Native black Briton*: I am home; I was born here.

Such a conversation, and certainly such a response, wraps the national boundary around the moral argument. We are dealing, it is thus claimed, with a domestic issue, in which ethnic *origin* is no more relevant than, say, colour of eyes or style of shoe. The claim being made is that 'being born here' radically alters the relationship between an old (white) and a new (coloured) Briton (and, perhaps, between an old Pakistani or Jamaican, and a new Pakistani or Jamaican). This is probably true – but not necessarily in the direction of greater unity. Under the aegis of multiculturalism, at least some ethnic minorities have received (and/or insisted upon and/or responded to) an invitation to construct a separate collective identity which, while 'British born', can only with some difficulty be regarded as participating fully in the British way of life. (The putative, and highly misleading, analogy is with the Welsh and Scots.)

There is the distinct possibility that the development of discrete, semi-official, ethnic minority 'sub-cultures', whether encouraged by indigenous multiculturalisms or generated by ethnic pride or religious imperialism (or by museums), may lead to centrifugal rather than centripetal tendencies – to a fragmentation of the nation. This is particularly likely when the minority 'identity' is tied to religion. As John Hinnells puts it: 'those of us who were active in the study of diaspora religions in the 1960s did not foresee the vitality and strength of the religions that would characterize these groups at the end of the millennium' (Hinnells, 2000: 10). Hinnells means that in a diaspora religions grow more, not less, religious; more, not less, exclusive – born in Britain, perhaps; but not of, or even for, Britain. This is obviously an outcome that will be determined by something more complex than a single strand of governmental or minority practice, or of the attitudes and behaviour of the white majority. As what is perhaps an extreme possibility, I offer the comments of a young Muslim British-born man. The example serves to make two points: (1) that being British born is no guarantee whatsoever of being loyally British; and (2) that, contrary to multicultural orthodoxies, ethnic minorities are neither all the same, nor all equally amiable, nor equally disposed to 'being British' – of which more in later chapters.

Aatish Taseer interviewed Hassan Butt, a 'British *Jihadist*' (the title of the interview) in August 2005. What follows is a paraphrase of a lengthy article. The 25-year-old Butt had helped recruit Muslims to fight in Afghanistan. He told Aatish Taseer that economic deprivation was not the reason for the disaffection of Pakistani youth:

> Most Pakistanis here are well established, they own their own homes, many have gone to University, they don't have any problems. . . I guess that's why the Pakistani youth are more responsive. Their elders came here for economic benefit, so they were a lot less willing to come out publicly with their opinions. . .[the youth] had everything they've needed and they're rejecting it. . .
>
> There is a difference between a citizen who is born in a country and someone who is here on a visa or a permit. Islamically, I agree that someone who runs from the middle east, where people like me are persecuted, and says 'Britain I want you to protect me' has entered a covenant of security. . .but most of our people, especially the youth, are British citizens. They owe nothing to the government. They did not ask to be born here; neither did they ask to be protected by Britain.

In answer to a question from Taseer as to whether they have any allegiance to the country, Butt replied: 'No, none whatsoever.' When asked if *he* felt any allegiance, he answered:

> I feel absolutely nothing for this country. . . The letter that was sent out by the Muslim Council of Britain to the mosques about how we should be spying on one another. I spoke to ten different imams. . .all ten disagreed with the letter, but they never publicly said so. . .
>
> One of the police officers [on a secretly taped BBC TV programme] said he would kill a Muslim if he could get away with it. And I do believe in my heart of hearts that the majority of British people – the majority being outside of London – would do that if they had the opportunity. . .
>
> (Interview in *Prospect*, August 2005)

A poll by Populus, published in *The Times* (7 February 2006), gave a figure of 12 per cent of 18–24-year-old Muslims as being of the view that suicide bombing in Britain was justified. Twelve per cent is several thousand people. Such people, and the alarmingly honest and awful Mr Butt, give the lie to one or two of the comforting fictions that have been spun around ethnic minority settlement in this country. Being British born does not mean being British. Poverty is not the mother of disaffection. Minorities are not all equal, and equally amiable. Muslims are not the same as Hindus and Rastafarians. Whites are neither wrong nor racist for saying so.

CHAPTER 7

MULTICULTURAL INDIA, MULTICULTURAL BRITAIN

Indians and democracy were made for each other.
Both are constructed to absorb a million mutinies, a
billion arguments. Indian democracy is the template
of the world's future.

(Tarun Tejpal, 2006)

India wants to build its future in the image of the
west. It is the overriding interest of those who share
such a view of the world to ensure a strong outpost
of western civilization among the people of non-
European descent as an alternative to future Muslim
civilization. (In the early seventies the western press
even discussed the desirability of India taking over
the Gulf.) Hence the convergence of interest of all
forces determined to contain and subvert the efforts
to create a civilization based on values other than
western.

(*Crescent International*, in Siddiqui, 1983: 262)

INTRODUCTION

There are obviously huge differences between India and
Britain. India is a country of well over a billion people; Great
Britain one of 60 million. India is a highly religious country,
predominantly Hindu, but one in which a variety of religions
compete for space and sound in a very public way. In Britain,
now barely Christian, the remaining worshippers practise
their mysteries in an almost furtive manner. Where Britain
is old, small, tired and cynical, India is huge, young (and
old!) and optimistic. In the Indian national election of 1996,

600 million electors made their choices from dozens of political parties: on average there were 26 candidates for each of the 543 national constituencies. At regional and communal level, Indian politics is more complicated again – as befits a country with 1,652 mother tongues (!), of which 22 are statutorily recognised. Britain is monolingual. Unlike Great Britain, India has a federal, written constitution, which means that the Indian courts frequently comment and rule on what we might regard as 'political' matters. (Although in Britain, of course, the introduction of the Human Rights Act has seen the British legal system increasingly likely to comment on political or 'constitutional' matters.)

The Preamble to the Indian Constitution (finally adopted in 1950) defines India as a 'sovereign, socialist, secular democratic republic'. Under this general stance, part of the complication of Indian politics lies in the caste system and the associated attempts to use the law and the public sector to 'positively discriminate' in favour of 'backward classes' of various types. In both India and Britain, these demands have been, or are being, institutionalised in a bureaucratic–legalistic way, the Indians being much further down this road than is Mr Blair's Britain. Thus, in an example provided by the website of the Indian National Commission for Backward Classes, in a hypothetical state with 10 million people, of whom 1 million are lower caste, and where there are 10,000 public sector jobs, 10 per cent (i.e. 1,000) of those jobs *must* go to the lower castes. India has, for some decades, had its National Commission for Backward Classes, and Britain now has a Commission for Equality and Human Rights. Both of these are involved in the business of 'positive discrimination'. In India, this involves trying to limit the public sector employment advantages of what are curiously known as the 'forward classes', and of applying a strict 'quota' system in favour of the 'backward', 'very backward' and 'other backward' classes or castes when it comes to filling jobs. A very large amount of government time and legal effort goes into trying to enforce these policies. To some commentators, such quota systems are both inefficient and open to corruption.

Even more curious than the 'backward' and 'forward' classes are the 'creamy layers' of the 'backward' and 'very backward' classes: 'creamy layers' are those members of the various backward classes who have, in fact, done very well out of the quota system in the public sector, and who maintain their positions by playing on their origins to mask their present advantage. With the Commission for Equality and Human Rights, a body recommended by the Parekh Commission, Britain is about to embark on a somewhat similar venture – and we are *absolutely* bound to get a large, self-indulgent, overpaid, over-protected creamy layer.

To return to India. While British politics has been relatively calm and corruption-free, Indian politics is vigorous, not to say violent. Early in 2006, in central Kerala, a march by the Muslim League led to the smashing up (allegedly by Muslims) of the printing presses of the Communist Party of India, which then led to the party calling everyone out on strike. In towns like Tellicherry and Kannur, nothing moved until or unless the CPI said so: threats, plus genuine support, effectively encouraged conformity. Some states (India has a federal constitution) are both unruly and corrupt, prone to serious and murderous inter-communal violence. In Jammu and Kashmir, and in some north-eastern regions, India faces serious separatist movements and consistent violence. In recent years, two Indian prime ministers have been assassinated: Indira Gandhi by her Sikh bodyguard, and Rajiv Gandhi, seemingly in response to the deployment of an Indian peace-keeping force in Sri Lanka (India's Tamil population having inevitably been caught up in the civil war in that neighbouring country). Crucially, India is home to about 150 million Muslims, almost more than there are in Pakistan, a Muslim state with which India has fought four wars and against whom India's nuclear weapons are deployed. The Muslims of independent India are as assertive as they were under British rule – and as assertive as they are now (and intend to be) in the UK.

For much of its post-Independence, post-Partition history, Indian politics was dominated, indeed held together, by

Congress, the party of the Nehrus and the Gandhis. Though the 'Hindu nationalist' party, the BJP (Bharatiya Janata Party), ruled in coalition in New Delhi from 1996–2004, in 2004 Sonia Gandhi's Congress Party became the largest single party. It now leads the United Progressive Alliance (to which 14 other parties belong) and has the informal support of the Communist Party of India (Marxist), the Communist Party of India, the Revolutionary Socialist Party and the Forward Bloc (once led by Sikh general Singh – see above). Prime Minister Manmohan Singh presides, therefore, over a government that is both an 'internal' and an 'external' coalition.

The United Progressive Alliance coalition functions only at the national level. At the state level, the same parties as make up Prime Minister Singh's coalition government are often enough in opposition, and even competition, rather than in coalition. The BJP, the opposition, also fought the 2004 election as part of a coalition. At the moment, then, Indian politics means sharp and shifting coalitions – a trend that is starting to be visible in Britain and a situation that is open to exploitation by determined minorities. We have already seen electoral fraud in Birmingham, and police investigations have been held in London. The relatively small size of British political parties makes them vulnerable to 'entryism' by sectional interests, and the Labour Party is already feeling the effect of this in certain of its constituencies. David Cameron seems to want, deliberately, to take his Conservative Party into the same quagmire.

So, with all the differences in size, structure and philosophy, there are at least three aspects to this Indian 'multiculturalism' that are, I think, relevant to our own situation. These are: (1) the matter of security and multiculturalism, in particular the position of the armed forces and the police; (2) the use of the public sector to drive forward a programme of positive discrimination, i.e. 'targets' or 'quotas'; and (3) the construction of 'citizenship' or 'socialisation' rituals and policies aimed at inculcating a loyalty to the nation, rather than to sectional interests.

MUSLIMS IN THE INDIAN ARMY: THE SACHAR COMMISSION

> India has more Muslims than Pakistan. But here is an interesting statistic from 9/11: there are no Indian Muslims that we know of in al-Qaeda and there are no Indian Muslims in America's post-9/11 prison camp. And no Indian Muslims have been found fighting alongside the jihadists in Iraq.
>
> (Friedman, 2006: 559)

At over 1 million men, the Indian Army is the third largest in the world. Every year 11.5 million Indian males become eligible (at 16) for military service, which is now voluntary. To the numbers in the regular army should be added well over 1 million paramilitaries, making the total number of Indians under arms the largest in the world. The paramilitary units, such as the Assam Rifles (41 battalions) or the Border Security Force (160 battalions), exist largely because local, 'communal' police forces are likely to be too 'communal' to be reliable. This, of course, elicits the counter-complaint (made frequently enough about Indian forces in Kashmir) that central forces are insufficiently 'communal', i.e. they are too brutal. 'Communal' can mean partisan; 'national' can mean alien.

'Communal' politics has, in the last year or so, achieved a particularly high level of saliency in India. This is because the absence of a solidly based national government has seen the Congress Party, in particular, 'bidding' for minority votes to buttress its hold on power. The Indian press refers to this process as one of creating 'vote banks'. The army now finds itself caught up in one of these bidding games.

In 2000, at Sonia Gandhi's insistence (she in turn responding to Muslim leaders), the government set up the Sachar Commission to examine the 'Social, Economic, and Educational Status of the Muslim Community of India'. This was clearly part of the 'vote banking' business, the Muslim League and other Muslim parties being part of Sonia's ruling coalition. Inevitably, therefore, such an inquiry would focus on the public sector, the location of patronage. Jobs in the public services (including the armed forces) in India are high status and well rewarded. Both under the British and in independent India, a policy of 'reservation' – in effect of 'positive discrimination' – sought to offset the poor economic performance of 'backward classes' of various types by reserving job quotas for them, the quotas being proportionate to their numbers in the general population. India has a great number of minorities – Ezhavas, Nadars, Dheevaras, Latin Catholics, 'scheduled caste' converts to Christianity, Muslims, Mapillas, Anglo-Indians. These 'backward classes', as they are called, seem to grow in number as their status is enhanced.

To date, these principles of quotas and reservation, in their full formal bureaucratic majesty, have not been officially extended to the armed forces. The Sachar Commission, however, in the process of gathering data on the general distribution of Muslims in the public services, asked the army chiefs for data on how many Muslims there were in the army. The demand caused uproar (*hungama*, as Indians have it) in the Lok Sabha, with shouting and pushing from the government's own coalition partners, as well as from the main opposition. Opposition leader L. K. Advani, accusing the government of 'vote bank politics', said: 'Is this a prelude to reservations in the Army on the basis of religion? It is the remedy worse than the disease' (*The Hindu*, 15 February 2006).

Army chiefs were appalled at the Sachar request. According to Chief of Army Staff, General J. J. Singh: 'We have never had this kind of a thing like where you come from, what language do you speak or what religion you believe in. . . We are apolitical, secular and we are a professional force' (*Mysore Mail*, 14 February 2006). Initially, the army said it did not keep such figures, and then that it did but that it would not hand them over. Then it agreed to give the data to the defence minister, but only on condition that they would not be forwarded to the Sachar Commission (*The Hindu*, 15 February 2006). They appealed to the commander in chief, the president of India, Dr Abdul Kalam, a Muslim. The *Sainik Kalyan Sangh* (the association of retired army officers) denounced both the government and the Sachar Commission,

121

although the All-India Muslim Women's Personal Law Board came out in favour of gathering the data (*Deccan Herald*, 16 February 2006). On a news website, retired Colonel Dr Anil Athale criticised the Sachar Commission for equating the armed forces with ordinary central government departments: 'In which other organisation is dying for the country part of the job?' he asked. He insisted that Sachar should be prohibited from gathering data on the armed forces, as this would be the 'thin end of the wedge', bringing vote-bank politics into security matters, and thus destroying the effectiveness of the Army and jeopardising national security. Colonel Athale addressed what was obviously a concern, though something he in fact dismissed – that Muslim troops could not be relied upon in India's main military deployment in Kashmir. He referred, in particular, to the reputed unreliability of Indian Army Muslim troops in the 1948 Indian action in Hyderabad (against a would-be separatist Muslim Nizam and his Muslim troops) and in the 1999 action in Kargil, against Pakistani troops and insurgents (Athale, 2006).

Colonel Athale and other military commentators denied that the argument had anything to do with an apparent decline in the proportion of Muslims – from 32 per cent in the (British) Indian Army, to the present level of 2.8 per cent, well below the 12 per cent of the Indian population that is Muslim (the figures for Sikhs seem to show a reduction from 30 per cent to 2 per cent). Military commentators saw this as reflecting nothing more than the result of the creation of Pakistan, when many Muslim regiments became part of the army of Pakistan, and of a post-Independence deployment strategy of moving away from 'a legacy, slowly being diluted, of combat arms or regiments recruiting from a particular zone or mixture of ethnic groups' (*ibid.*). The BJP leader, and leader of the opposition in the Lok Sabha, L. K. Advani, said that 'The Army has no religion. Selections in the Army are based on the ability to defend the country' (*The Hindu*, 15 February 2006). On the other hand, the Sikh separatist organisation, the Khalistan Affairs Centre, stated that, for five decades, the Indian Army had been 'culling' Muslims and Sikhs; and that there was no future in 'dynastic oligarchic Indian *demoNocracy*' for Sikhs and Muslims (Khalistan Affairs Center, 2006).

That the army had reason to be worried about the Sachar Commission being the 'thin end of the wedge' may perhaps be seen from two submissions to the Commission by leading Muslims. There was general complaint about the poor educational and economic position of Muslims, about the 2002 'genocide' in Gujarat, about the lack of good, free schools and universities, about segregation of Muslims in poor neighbourhoods. As a solution, the petitioners told the Sachar Commission that there should be reserved jobs in general, and in educational institutions in particular. Government funding for Muslim schools should be both generous and free from quality regulation. There should be government interest-free loans for Muslim enterprises. Police and employment exchange officers should set up special camps for Muslims *before* any public sector recruitment campaigns started, to make sure they got in quickly. In any career, Muslims who got a job on merit should not count against the reserved quota. There should be special classes in English and computing for Muslims. The police should have Muslims in proportion to their numbers. In Gujarat, the Public Services Commission should examine why Muslims do not appear in sufficient numbers. Houses should be built for Muslims, free land should be provided, and banks should be made to open up in Muslim areas (*Sunday Pioneer, Kochi,* 26 February 2006; *Milli Gazette* online, 5 March 2006).

This very broad range of demands was not acceptable to R. Alemelu, of Coimbatore, writing in *The Hindu*. As he wrote: 'That Muslims are backward cannot be denied. But their backwardness is not historical like that of the Scheduled Castes and the Scheduled Tribes. Muslims have remained backward because their community is not open to reforms' (*The Hindu*, 28 February 2006). Raghavendra R., of Bangalore, was even more forthright: 'The Union Government order to recruit Muslims into the armed forces is ridiculous. Muslims are a minority community, which demanded a separate state and divided the country. Muslims should develop true patriotism for the country. No other country has been so accommodative to them' (*The Hindu*, 17 February 2006).

The issue raised by the Sachar Commission and addressed in the response by India's senior military is that of the existence within a nation state of a relatively small but very vocal minority – in this case Muslims – whose sense of being members of a wider community (the Islamic *ummah*) leads at least some Indians to worry about their loyalty. India has very serious security problems on much of its northern frontier, and a long-standing confrontation with Muslim Pakistan. Pakistan's army is nearly all Muslim. Both India and Pakistan are nuclear powers. Iran may become another Muslim nuclear power in India's 'backyard'. China is an ever-present threat, constructing roads, railways and pipelines in a huge arc over the top of India; and China has also been a major supplier of weapons to Pakistan. The Great Game is now being played for much higher stakes, and with much bigger armies and far more lethal armaments than it ever was before. The seemingly innocuous business of 'counting' the number of Muslims in the Indian Army is really a question of fear about army loyalty and morale, no matter how much India's multiculturalists, and Muslims perhaps, may want to see it merely as one of quotas and equal opportunities. Muslims, of course, point to Hindu (or other) expressions of this fear as, in itself, evidence of 'exclusion', and insist that the army's impartiality is compromised if it does not properly represent Muslims. Mr Ghulam Muhammed, writing to the *Indian Express*, said that the Indian Army had been responsible for the massacre of 7,000 Muslims in Assam, and that the army would not fire upon rioting Hindus when they attacked Muslims. 'The disenchantment of Muslims from the political processes was', he wrote, 'more dangerous for the integrity and security of the nation than the head count of Muslims in the Army' ('Demographics of the Armed Forces', 2006). Other correspondents indicated that, as of May 2006, the Sachar Commission had been 'warned off' by the most senior politicians, responding to army pressure.

The Indian Army is not alone, of course, in being concerned about morale. British military deployment to Iraq raised questions both about Muslim members of the British Army, and about British Muslims taking part in *jihad* action against that army. Internally, British police forces, increasingly involved in policing 'terrorism', are being 'racialised' – subject to the 'equal opportunities' policies of the Race Relations (Amendment) Act 2000 and the associated Equality Act. Both India and Britain, then, seem to have a problem of the existence within the state of minorities whose loyalties do not, perhaps, derive fully and exclusively from membership of that state. Conversely, such minorities may – and, in India, clearly do – feel threatened when and if 'excluded'. For both countries, this is a major security issue.

CREAMY LAYERS AND SPONGING THE QUOTA

Both countries have a problem in maintaining political and social stability in the context of a fragmented, or fractious, political culture. Indian politics *is* coalition politics; British politics is moving in that direction. Agitating and exacerbating this fragmentation, in India and in Britain, are the demands made by multiculturalists, that there should be 'fair shares' for, or 'positive discrimination' in favour of, a whole congeries of minorities. In India, these policies of what is called 'reservation' both pre-date Independence and have been a source of argument and dispute ever since.

In the year 2000, that is 50 years after Independence, the government of the southern state of Kerala appointed a three-man commission, chaired by Justice K. K. Narendran

> to study and report on the adequacy or otherwise of representation of the backward classes in the service under the State Government, public sector undertakings, autonomous bodies and institutions under the State Government including the Universities.

Kerala has a very large public sector, absorbing much of the budget of the State. The Narendran Commission took the

straightforward view that where, say, a 'scheduled caste con-
verted to Christianity', and was one of the 'backward classes',
and if it was 5 per cent of the general population, then it
should show up in the various public sector employment centres as having 5 per cent of the jobs. There was some debate:
did this mean that such a caste could have *only* 5 per cent?
What happens to a 'reserved' job left vacant, where there is no
'backward class' person to fill it? Such issues (with which our
own public sector will soon have the happy fortune to struggle) clearly caused the Commission some internal controversy.
It was 'solved' as follows:

> We were handling a subject which has almost
> always raised conflicting views and social discomfort
> in the State. To our tremendous satisfaction
> bordering on a little pride we can say we have
> worked as a team. . . This is perhaps because all the
> three of us are grandfathers; and we would like to
> believe that in this wonderful State and country,
> where our grandchildren and their generation have
> the good fortune to live, there is absolutely no need
> for carrying difference of opinion on even the most
> sensitive issues to a point beyond the limit of healthy
> debate and generous consensus.
>
> (Narendran, 2004: 62)

However, the good sense of grandfathers was ignored;
and the publication of the Narendran Report inevitably gave
rise to argument, discussion and debate about its implemen-
tation, about its methodology, and about issues such as the
'creamy layer', those reasonably well-off members of a backward class who had somehow got a permanent grip on some
well-paid jobs. Not too much attention was paid to the issue
of the sense of regarding public sector employment as a tool
of social engineering, although the Commission itself said that

> Without the benefit of reservation, no community
> among the backward classes can have adequate

representation in the services [under scrutiny]. . .
Even with reservation, most of the communities are
not getting adequate representation in all the
categories of posts. We conclude the report by
pointing out that the reservation for Backward
Classes is only a means to an end and not an end in
itself. It cannot be a permanent feature.

(ibid.: 61)

The last sentence must be destined to join the Indian collection of famous last words. The United Democratic Front
government of Kerala (a coalition) retained support of 'communal' parties only by accepting the system of 'reserved' quotas and promising to do things like preventing a vacant post
that 'belonged' to a particular backward class from being
transferred to another backward class – or to the general
'merit quota', i.e. the reserved quotas are not to be counted
against any of the actual jobs the particular backward class
may have won 'on merit'. There were certainly changes in
employment practices in the public sector. The *New Indian
Express* stated (15 February 2006) that, of the 402 Keralan
teachers whose jobs had been 'regularised', 112 were Muslims
and another 193 came from one single district of the state.
Guesses were made as to the nature of the processes behind
such an outcome.

Public sector employment is highly sought after in Kerala.
The average wage for bus drivers in the Keralan State Road
Transport Corporation (the bus system, with 30,000 employees) is three times the average wage in the private bus system.
The Indian journal *Frontline* (April 2006) stated that, while
the Indian PSUs (Public Sector Undertakings) received 40 per
cent of national gross capital investment, they produced but
25 per cent of output, and had a rate of return of capital
of one tenth that of the private sector. The international
Transparency Index gives evidence of widespread bribe-
taking in the public sector, costing the Indian economy many
millions of rupees. It is, for example, relatively easy to forge
the identity papers needed to 'make' you one of the backward

classes, which are defined by name. The *Times of India* drew attention to the substantial scope for corruption implicit in the quota system, commenting, in particular, that 'the creamy layer of all groups who sponge the quota should be excluded from both Scheduled Castes and Scheduled Tribes as well as from Other Backward Classes'. A young Indian girl commented that making a job application in such a system is like entering a race in which the quota candidates are already past the winning post (*Times of India*, 26 April 2006).

Could 'sponging the quota' and 'creamy layers' become part of life for some of the 6 million UK public sector employees? Or will our own Commission for Equality and Human Rights (CEHR) make sure that they won't? Will it simply do its job, and then wind itself up? The Commission for Racial Equality, soon to be the Commission for Equality and Human Rights, has produced a list of 43,000 public bodies duty bound to 'make the promotion of racial equality central' to their life and work: targets first, quotas next? The CEHR has yet to get to work, but the Equality Act 2006 is in force, producing documents such as the May 2006 Home Office consultation document *Public Service Agreement – Community Safety and Justice 2008/9 to 2010/11*, and is already at work on what it calls 'perception targets'. An example:

A.2.5. . . . Tackling inequalities and opening
opportunities for inclusion, building a more representative
public sector workforce, including within the Home
Office, and integrating newcomers into British society.

To date, of course, whether in the public sector or anywhere else, employers have done everything they can to make sure that their employees are *not* representative of the general population, believing that plumbers, for example, would be best at plumbing, and intelligent plumbers would be better than lazy ones; and the same goes for academics, police, ministers of religion and ministers of the Crown. Perhaps we, too, will need grandfathers like Mr Justice Narendran.

INDIA IS MY COUNTRY: *JAI HIND!*

The third matter in which we share both problem and experience with India is the age-old question of social stability. How do we, and how does India, elaborate and propagate a set of shared civic values – a sense, that is, of being a nation? India has a clear policy – clearer, perhaps, than the inconclusive musings of Gordon Brown (Brown, 2006), or the diffidence we see in British schools and churches about becoming anything other than shy and awkward about celebrating national days and national events.

'Citizenship' discussions are going on in several European countries. The Dutch, for example, have produced, as a citizenship 'test', a DVD depicting, amongst other things, a topless female and two men kissing (there is, apparently, a properly Dutch way of reacting to such images). Germany has a 'test' that seeks views on forced marriage and homosexuality. The English, seeking 'Englishness', are experimenting with photographs of a cup of tea and of a London bus (since taken out of service). However ludicrous some of these things may seem, countries in Western Europe are at least beginning to realise that 'multiculture' may be as much a problem as a Good Thing.

India is indeed, as Tejpal has said, a miracle 'constructed to absorb a million mutinies, a billion arguments'. It is kept together, he says, because it has a 'timeless philosophy', of Hindu provenance. He may be overstating this: it was, and is, the very power of Hinduism to which Muslims objected when they sought and obtained Partition. British India's Muslims, of course, saw Partition as the only possible response to Hindu triumphalism. Conversely, and in some ways like Britain, India is a democracy in which democratic values are only too easily exploited by minorities that are neither democratic by inclination nor exclusively loyal to the country in which they live. India has considerable experience of dealing with this problem; experience which derives, indeed, from the days before Independence. From its inception, India has known and faced such an issue. In part, the Indian response has been to rely on its radically decentralised political system to manage – by permitting – considerable latitude in inter-regional, inter-ethnic and inter-religious dispute and conflict. The natural condition of India's constitution is a permanent state of crisis management, and after 50 years they are quite good at it. Under the engagingly cheerful names of 'stirs' or 'agitations', Indians tolerate a level of street politics that would be classified as riot in Britain and Western Europe.

At the back of all this, though, is a resolute reliance on old-fashioned socialisation (brainwashing, to us?) to create, especially in the young, a sense of national unity. In ways now unthinkable to the sneering scepticisms of self-obsessed, self-abasing Europeans, India's leaders promote the practice of patriotism, of love of country. Indian children start every school day with the 'General Pledge':

INDIA IS MY COUNTRY
India is my country.
All Indians are my brothers and sisters.
I love my country and I am proud of its rich and varied
heritage. I shall always strive to be worthy of it.
I shall give my parents, teachers and all elders respect
and treat everyone with courtesy.
To my country and my people I pledge my devotion. In
their well-being and prosperity alone lies my happiness.

This is said every day by the 190 million children who attend India's schools. They stand in rows, arms outstretched, saying these extraordinary words. I would draw the reader's attention to the use of the word 'alone' in the last sentence. For comparison, here is the American Pledge of Allegiance, used in all US schools:

I Pledge Allegiance to the flag of the United States of
America and to the Republic for which it stands, one
Nation under God, Indivisible, with Liberty and Justice
for all.

Note how much wider than 'mere' patriotism is the Indian Pledge. Every school day ends with the singing of the National Anthem:

Thou art the ruler of the minds of all people,
Dispenser of India's destiny.
Thy name arouses the hearts of the Punjab,
Sind, Gujarat and Maratha,
Of the Dravida and Orissa and Bengal.
It echoes in the hills of the Vindhyas and Himalayas,
Mingles in the music of the Jamuna and the Ganges
And is chanted by the waves of the Indian Sea.
They pray for the blessings and sing thy praise.
The saving of all people waits in thy hand,
Thou dispenser of India's destiny,
Victory, victory, victory to thee.

As if this were not enough, India has great national celebrations: Republic Day (26 January) and Martyrs' Day (30 January) held in the capital, with smaller versions held at state and local levels. The Republic Day parade in New Delhi is the world's greatest military spectacular – and, apart from anything else, it underscores the fact that India's military are under civilian control, a rare occurrence in the post-imperial world.

India's school textbooks are unabashedly patriotic – without being (except occasionally!) biased:

A good citizen is conscious of his duties as well as
rights. . . A good citizen obeys the laws of the land. . .
he is loyal to the government of the country and is
always mindful of the interests and welfare of his
country. . . Our symbols remind us that we should
love our motherland and display qualities of
sacrifice, hard work, and steadfastness. Above all,
we should be truthful. We should resolve to work
for the prosperity of our country.
(*Social Studies Today*, Book Four, National Council
of Educational Research and Training, and the Indian
Council for Indian School Certificate Exams)

It would be silly to pretend that Indian society is without very serious internal conflict. However, there is also evidence of that most remarkable and rare achievement – a coherent basic culture. In 2005 and 2006, the weekly journal *India Today* ran two surveys of young urban India, i.e. of Indians aged 18–35, of whom there are 250 million. Seventy per cent of Indians, i.e. 730 million people, are under 34. These are the most 'modern' Indians, all born well after Independence, for whom the wicked British and heroic freedom fighters are encountered in textbooks, on statues and during ceremonies, not in 'real' life.

From the 2006 special edition of *India Today*, we learn that 74 per cent of such Indians believe that their vote made a difference in Indian democracy, though 68 per cent felt that corruption was the greatest ill facing India. Some 88 per cent said that, if asked, they would volunteer to serve in the army, should India find itself in a war situation. In all, 86 per cent felt that men and women were given equal status and opportunity; 80 per cent said that sex before marriage was wrong, and 73 per cent that arranged marriages were more likely to be successful than ones decided by 'love'. Some 57 per cent of men and 13 per cent of women had watched pornography; 62 per cent visited a place of worship at least once a week, while only 3 per cent said that they never did; 68 per cent preferred to live in a joint family, and 31 per cent in a nuclear family.

The 2005 survey showed that the majority of young Indians preferred to work and live in India, not abroad. Again, a substantial majority (82 per cent) would serve at times of war; 71 per cent would not countenance putting elderly relatives in an old people's home.

Even given the vagaries and duplicities of such opinion polls, such a set of comments indicates a solid basis for Indian national and civil society. Indians are religious in ways that have long since disappeared from Europe (though not from America). In accepting, it seems, arranged marriage, joint family residence and responsibility for and to the elderly, they exemplify the civic virtues spelt out in the Pledge made every day in school. In a country for which war is an ever-present reality, not a distant memory or remote possibility, the very high level of willingness to serve in such wars indicates not only the strength of patriotism but also (again!) how different India is from Britain (perhaps) and Europe (certainly).

To repeat: India, since its inception, has been a society more prone to centrifugal than centripetal forces. It maintains, within its national boundaries, conflicting forces that would make lesser societies fall apart. Indian survival and success may well be due to the extraordinary nature of its main religion, Hinduism, or because of (generally!) very skilful national politicians. Among those skills, and among the better of its religious virtues, are those that emphasise the civic virtues of mutuality and decency. No one, in India or elsewhere, should think that the task of nation-making is a one-off business. In India, unlike the UK or Western Europe, the enactment of daily, and annual, rituals states very clearly that 'loyalty', in the broadest sense of that word, is something that is neither natural nor to be taken for granted. There is no out-there nation to which something called 'loyalty' can be attached by command. Loyalty has to be made, day by day, by those concerned in making it and in being it: and this is where India has (against the odds) been so remarkably successful.

CONCLUSION

This may all seem far removed from 'multicultural Britain'. Yet we face similar demands for the 'communalisation' of the police service; and in its absence we have already experienced a functional equivalent in 'no-go' areas in towns in the Midlands. The Macpherson Report managed to convince everyone that the police were all racists; various ethnically based groups exist in the police to, it seems, counter this alleged 'racism'. More importantly, in all likelihood, future deployments of British (or Western) military forces will lead them into areas in which Islam – and perhaps Hinduism – is a major factor. We have already seen this in the matter of Iraq. There may, indeed are, arguments about weapons of mass destruction, or UN resolutions, or how best (if at all) to 'deal with' the Saddam Husseins of the world. For 'British' Muslims, however, the reason for opposing the war in Iraq was simple: it was because they are Muslims and so are the Iraqis. They see Anglo-American military action in (on, even) Iraq as war against an Islamic country, on 'fellow' Muslims. British 'national interest' either comes second or is subsumed into a general pro-Muslim foreign policy. Indian Army chiefs and Indian politicians face the same problem that we do: how far can 'multiculturalism' be indulged before it jeopardises national security? In the UK, both major parties are seeing their electoral base eroded, from within or without, by elements of multiculturalism. The ensuing 'coalition' politics may well paralyse our foreign policy.

India has many lessons for us and for our understanding of our own problems of multiculturalism. Where are our national symbols and celebrations? Do we really need 'targets' and 'quotas' in the public sector (or the private), and should the armed forces be subject to such policies? How do we get away from the view that we are so secure in war-weary Western Europe that we can afford to deconstruct and thereby destroy the bases of national loyalty? I will turn to these issues in the last chapter of this book.

CHAPTER 8

ISLAM

I had no intention of writing a separate chapter on Islam, or on Hinduism, or any other discrete religious or ethnic minority: this is a book about multiculturalism. Yet such a book would be very, very different 'without', as it were, Islam. The same can be said, obviously, for, say, Hinduism or black Caribbean communities: but on a very different plane. The issues raised by bombs on London buses are not the same as those raised by Diwali or the Notting Hill Carnival. Another reason for avoiding saying much about Islam is fear. For the first time in my life I find myself writing with, somewhere in my mind, a wary feeling that critical comment on Islam could result in threats and violence coming my way. My wife feels the same. Another reason is that comments about Islam are, in fact, to be found throughout this book – it is the salient fact, or most explicit rhetoric, or most vociferous presence in multiculturalism. After mulling all that over, then, I do feel it necessary to make two or three comments on Islam.

> The world of Islam is vibrating in this end of the twentieth century as it was vibrating at the end of the seventh; God is witness of this strength of faith. The mosques open up, the roads are mosques, and the earth is a mosque. The Umma is here; the rich and the poor, the computer scientist and the unlettered, witnesses of the same testimony, looking to quench the same thirst.
>
> (Ramadan, 2001)

On the night of 1 May 2006, a Channel Four *Dispatches* programme was presented by Dr Tariq Ramadan, quoted above. He described himself as a European Muslim. Dr Ramadan takes the view that it is *in Europe* that Islam will, through the Islamic scriptural exegetical technique or intellectual endeavour known as *ijtihad*, achieve an 'Islamic Reformation'. Through *ijtihad*, he said, the teachings of the Qur'an and of the *hadith* could be, and should be, 'contextualised'. In one of his books, Ramadan defines *ijtihad* as 'a vision of history which, at each stage, refers man to his points of reference and to their interpretation in order to find a forward solution, but one which legitimates its link with the original orientation' (Ramadan, 2001: 95). The television programme documented his travels round various European countries, and then Pakistan, as he put this point of view to several Muslim imams and gatherings. It has to be said that, with the exception of a group of Muslim women, he got a fairly frosty reception, summed up perhaps in the stinging comment from one man that he, Tariq Ramadan, had a 'colonised mind'.

During Dr Ramadan's visit to Denmark, he interviewed a young male Muslim who had taken a leading role in the violent Muslim reaction to the infamous (or famous) cartoons, the so-called 'incendiary cartoons'. These cartoons apparently depict the prophet Mohammed as carrying a bomb on his head. Like many people, I have never seen them, as they have been taken out of circulation by a terrorised press. Ramadan's interlocutor had no problem at all with the worldwide violence and deaths that had occurred; and he felt that in such ways would the West begin to understand Islam. Indeed.

As the quote from Ramadan's book indicates, and as the response to his televised journey shows, Islam does not consider itself as in any sense a minority: 'the basic resource of the Islamic movement is its size' (Siddiqui, 1983: 19). The *ummah* is the dominant loyalty. In the *ummah*, by definition, Muslims are not just the majority but the totality. The *ummah* is not just of today, but is (see the Ramadan quote at the beginning of this chapter) all the things that Islam ever was. The fierce pride in the sheer scale of the Muslim historical accomplishment (as well as exaggerations of it) is matched only by sorrow and fury at what is considered to be its present degraded state. Since the West is generally blamed for this degradation, then this fury – writ large or small, a grumble, a growl or a roar of revenge – identifies us Westerners as the problem and the enemy. Muslim history seeks to reverse this: *Muslim history is Now*. Dr Kalim Siddiqui, founder-director of the Muslim Institute tells us:

> Despite the tragedy of Spain (1610), according to A J P Taylor, the celebrated English historian, the European civilization did not really get going until the twentieth century. In other words, the civilization of Islam did not finally lose its dominance within itself and in relation to the competing environmental civilization until the early part of this [twentieth] century.
>
> (Siddiqui, 1983: 5)

Kalim Siddiqui, now deceased, was an important British-based Muslim intellectual leader. The 'tragedy of Spain', and the solution, is dealt with in another book:

> The rigid orthodoxy of the Official Roman Catholic Church in Spain during the seventeenth century transformed the Iberian peninsula into an economic and a spiritual wilderness. . . Today there are again Muslims in Andalus and their numbers are growing. One of the meanings of Andalus in Arabic is 'to become green at the end of the summer' – and insh'Allah the long dry summer of the last five centuries in Europe is drawing to its close.
>
> (Thomson and Muhammad 'Ata' Ur'Rahim, 2004: 262)

If history is there to be repealed, as it were, then, by the same token, it is unlikely that Muslims will ever adapt to that quintessentially Western political lifestyle, the nation state.

Kalim Siddiqui again quotes, with obvious approval, Abul Ala Maudoodi's insistence that 'It is difficult to imagine how a nationalist State based on western democracy can be instrumental for Islamic State' (Siddiqui, 1983: 12–13); and he has this to say, also:

> The Islamic State is the Muslim's natural habitat and their dependence on the Islamic State is as complete as that of a fish in water. If Muslims survive without the Islamic State they survive like fish in a bowl of water or in an aquarium. . .denied their freedom. . . A State that is dependent for survival on the traditional enemies of Islam cannot be an Islamic State.
>
> (*ibid.*: 9)

The very notions of the *ummah* and the principles of the nation state (*any* nation state) are difficult to reconcile. While Muslims living in a Muslim country, such as Pakistan or Saudi Arabia, may (may!) live within a congruency (more or less) of nation and religion, this is much less likely to be the case with Muslims in Britain (or other European countries), where there is no such congruency. Dr Siddiqui has some harsh things to say about the Gulf States ('Saudi Arabia has the most corrupt rulers of any Muslim State ever') and about 'second-generation Islamicists' in Europe. He has good things to say only about Iran (*ibid.*: 12). There are, to Dr Siddiqui's mind, very few countries where the *ummah* and a nation state sit down easily and nicely together. In documents such as those produced by the Islamic Human Rights Commission in 2004, or by the Muslim Council of Britain in 2005, we see a group, defined by its faith, laying out the terms, or boundaries rather, of its presence here in Britain.

In Dr Ramadan's television programme, it was noticeable that, while there was an awareness of differences between, say, Britain and France (France not too good), when it came to it, Dr Ramadan ended by asking his fellow Muslims to see themselves as part of 'Europe' rather than of a particular country – such, indeed, is his main message. It is also a way of avoiding the hard fact of present-day life in Europe: that, in spite of all efforts to the contrary, we still live in nation states, to which we owe our loyalty. Dr Ramadan is of Egyptian provenance, was born in Switzerland (to where his father had fled to avoid Egyptian government threats to the Muslim Brotherhood), is resident in Britain, easily bilingual, and is married to a Frenchwoman. *To Be a European Muslim* (1999) was his earliest book. Despite the strictures of Dr Siddiqui, the *ummah*, like Dr Ramadan and multiculturalism in general, would be more at ease in a soft-state no-state 'Europe' than it is, or could be, in single hard-state nations like France or the United Kingdom. Perhaps the dissolution of Europe's nation states is what is required for Dr Ramadan's 'Islamic Reformation'.

The Great Cartoon Riots tell us two things: first, that Muslim threats work and that many in the West will chicken out; and second, that Western notions of the distinction between, say, the public and the private, or between government and society, are little understood or simply not familiar in the non-Western world. This applies to non-Western Muslims and non-Muslims alike. I was in India when the Great Cartoon Riots broke out. If the Indian English-language press is anything to go by, then the following letter (which was fairly typical) by a Hindu correspondent shows how far apart the 'West and the Rest' are:

Those in politics and the media should display greater restraint while dealing with sensitive issues. Muslims have been hurt by the cartoons published in the European media. The governments concerned should apologise.

(*The Hindu*, 10 February 2006)

I stress that this letter is by a Hindu. Non-Western societies generally have difficulty with several things we simply take for granted: the distinction between the public and the private, between acts of the state and the acts of an individual or of the private sector; between religion *in* society and the religion *of* a society; between the freedoms of the citizen and the responsibility of the government. Such things, part and parcel of normal civic life in the post-Locke, post-J. S. Mill world, are not so deeply or widely held in societies beyond the reach of those authors and traditions. While many letters and much comment in the Indian English-language press deplored the violence, which claimed over 100 lives in over 50 countries, there was much less inclination to see the cartoons as the sole responsibility of one small privately owned newspaper in one small northern European state. The foreign ministries of 11 Islamic states demanded action from the Danish government; and 17 Islamic states called for the Danish government to punish the editor of *Jyllands-Posten*, the newspaper that published the cartoons. The Organization of the Islamic Conference and the Arab League demanded that the UN impose international sanctions on Denmark, prompting the Danish prime minister to say that this was the worst crisis in Denmark since World War Two! George Bush and Condoleezza Rice were blamed and burned in effigy: and, in what may seem like an unexpected and grotesque twist, a spokesperson for Darfur (of all places!) declared that the Swedish foreign minister was unwelcome in his homeland. All this is incredible to Western European minds, even those few that retain religious beliefs: where Muslims believe in Islam, Christians – in Europe anyway – only practise Christianity. There has been considerable discussion in Britain recently over the *Da Vinci Code* – a silly book and an even sillier film, in which, among other things, Jesus is depicted as having children by a 'prostitute', the much maligned Mary Magdalene. Again quite recently the *Jerry Springer Show*, on at the Theatre Royal, Newcastle, depicted Jesus as a large 'gay' baby in a nappy. The comment of two of the North East's bishops on the *Da Vinci Code* film and book was that so long as people were 'talking about Jesus', then fine. It is hard to imagine a Muslim imam taking such a relaxed and permissive attitude to the *Satanic Verses* or the *Jyllands-Posten* cartoons.

This chapter started with a discussion of the hopes of Dr Tariq Ramadan that it would be in Europe that Islam is able both to find its liberal self and to help transform Europe into something compatible with that liberalism. I have to say that Tariq Ramadan is a brave and persistent man. I heard him speak at a 24 July 2005 conference at the Islamic Centre in Regent's Park, London. Ramadan told a gathering of several hundred Muslims (mostly men) that they should learn about British history, culture and literature; Western Muslims should, he said, embrace Western culture. He clearly knew, when he remonstrated with (rather than merely advised) his listeners, that he had an uphill task. Speaking to them very directly, he said: 'This is your country. You are British citizens. Be British Muslim citizens. How can you live with people you do not know?'

Ramadan instanced Islamic bookshops: there was nothing in them, he said, about the country in which his audience lived. I went to the bookshop that is part of the Islamic Centre. Its stock was, indeed, all about Islam; nothing at all about the West. Fair enough, perhaps. There were, though, two books on Christianity: *Christianity and Islam, According to the Bible and the Qur'an*, and *Christianity, the Original and the Present Reality*. Both derive from Saudi Arabia. In one, the Saudi publishers state that their aim is 'to open the Christians' eyes to the true reality of their erroneous beliefs'. The other lists the errors of the Bible, contrasting these with the rectitude of the Qur'an, and concluding with various comments, such as that the Bible is full of 'monumental errors' and 'The Bible I always heartily disliked. . .one felt disgusted and saddened instead of being helped and comforted' (Al-Moghamis, 2002; As-Saheem, 1999). On returning home, I checked the Christian bookshops in Newcastle: they either had no books on Islam, or, where they did, they were academic, 'secular', dispassionate treatments of Islam. All there was in the Regent's Park bookshop about the main religion of the country in which Muslims live, and of which many of them are citizens, were two anti-Christian books. It is not surprising that Tariq Ramadan felt obliged to say to his Muslim audience that, deep in their hearts, they did not trust their hosts. He was right.

What more can one say about Islam? It writes its own record in a very vigorous, not to say violent, way. In another pleasant little book I picked up at the Regent's Park Islamic Centre, I learnt:

> So when you meet (in fight – Jihad in Allah's cause)
> those who disbelieve, smite at their necks till you
> have killed and wounded many of them, then bind a
> bond firmly (on them, i.e. take them as captives).
> Thereafter (is the time for) either generosity (i.e. free
> them without ransom) or ransom (according to what
> benefits Islam), until war lays down its burden.
>
> (Humaid, 1995: 32)

Over a hundred years before, and on a very different continent, and in a very different culture, a similar definition of Muslim 'exceptionalism' was offered by one of British India's Muslim leaders:

> Suppose that the English community and their army
> were to leave India, taking with them all their
> cannons and their splendid weapons and all else,
> who then would be the rulers of India? Is it possible
> that under these circumstance two nations – the
> Mohammedans and the Hindus – could sit on the
> same throne and remain equal in power? Most
> certainly not. It is necessary that one of them should
> conquer the other. To hope that both could remain
> equal is to desire the impossible and the
> inconceivable. At the same time you must remember
> that although the number of Mohammedans is less
> than that of the Hindus, and although they contain
> far fewer people who have received a higher English
> education, yet they must not be considered
> insignificant or weak. Probably by themselves they

would be enough to maintain their position. But
suppose they were not. Then our Muslim brothers,
the Pathans, would come out as a swarm of locusts
from their mountain valleys, and make rivers of
blood to flow from their frontier on the north to the
extreme end of Bengal. This thing – who after the
departure of the English would be conquerors would
rest on God's will. But until one nation has
conquered the other and made it obedient, peace
cannot reign in the land.

(Speech advising Muslims not to join the Indian
'National Congress' [called the 'Bengali Assembly'
by the speaker] by Sir Syed Ahmed Khan,
at Meerut, 16 March 1888, in Khan, 1998)

I am not alone in thinking that trouble is on its way.
Anthony Glees and Chris Pope have provided ample evidence
of Muslim involvement in terrorist and extremist networks in
British universities (Glees and Pope, 2005). I have already
quoted the views of Hassan Butt, the 'British *Jihadist*'. If
Muslims wish to live in peace in Great Britain, as well as in
freedom, then they have a lot of work to do – among themselves. As Tariq Ramadan expostulated to his audience at the
(post-bomb) 2005 conference at the Regent's Park Mosque:
How can you live among people you do not know? The
'people' to whom he was referring were us, the British.
The people he was addressing were, I assume, the proverbial
moderate Muslims.

To conclude on a more cheerful note. A Bangladeshi taxi
driver who took me from Hackney to the Regent's Park
Mosque seemed to know perfectly well where and among
whom he lived; and I leave the last words to him. He was curious to know why I was going to the Regent's Park Mosque,
for he never went there. Most Bangladeshis, he said, like
England and London, as the UK and Edward Heath had supported Bangladesh in its war with Pakistan; and now America
and the UK were doing what they could to help economically,
whereas Arabs are no help:

I am a Muslim and I have nothing in common with those rich Arabs, never go to their mosques; in Saudi Arabia they call us Bangladeshis 'beggars'. We are pro-British, and if I don't like British foreign policy I can change it through elections – or go somewhere else.

His son, he said, had a serious medical problem, and they got the best medical attention in England – much better than in Bangladesh. He had many good English friends: his family had good friends, and in the UK it was never 'oi, you, Muslim! What're you doing here?' Whereas in Saudi it was always 'You, you are a Bangladeshi.'

Suicide is not Islamic; nor is killing. There is no terror in the Qur'an. My taxi driver had no Arabic, though his sons were being taught it in the mosque. 'We are against terror, against killing. We are British.' Here we have at least one Muslim aware of – and grateful for – the blessing of living in Great Britain; a Muslim clearly unimpressed by Sura 4, 139/40 of the Qur'an, which urges Muslims to have no friends among the Unbelievers.

CHAPTER 9

MULTICULTURAL COLLAPSE

Commission for Equality and Human Rights:
JUSTICE, EQUALITY AND FAIRNESS. Chair,
salary highly competitive, Commissioners, attractive
remuneration plus expenses.

(Job advertisement, Spring 2006)

Championing equality, diversity and human rights in
modern Britain: the establishment of the new
Commission for Equality and Human Rights
(CEHR) is a major step forward in the
Government's broad agenda of delivering prosperity
and fairness for all. With the recent passing of the
Equality Act, and work progressing on the
Discrimination Law Review, and Equalities Review,
we are building a new comprehensive framework to
challenge inequality and disadvantage.

(*ibid.*)

I haven't the faintest idea.
(Mr David Roberts, Director, Enforcement and
Removals, Immigration and Nationality Directorate
of the Home Office, on being asked how many
people were in Britain illegally)

Seventy per cent of the British say that their everyday experience of immigrants is 'positive'. This is only slightly less than the average for eight European countries. It is higher than the particular response rate for any of the eight countries, apart from Sweden and Switzerland. Some 86 per cent of the British feel that religious leaders who advocate terrorism should be thrown out of the country, the figure for Spain and Germany being 93 per cent (*Daily Telegraph*, 5 January 2006). In another poll, 76 per cent of the British wanted a yearly limit on immigration, with only 4 per cent being strongly opposed; 69 per cent were worried that Britain was losing its culture (*Daily Telegraph*, 3 April 2006). In another poll, 80 per cent felt that police and politicians were too tolerant of Muslims, and 86 per cent that Muslim protests over the 'Danish' cartoons were a 'gross over-reaction'. Some 87 per cent expected another terrorist act like the 7 July 2005 bombings in London by four Muslim men (YouGov poll, *Vijay Times*, 14 February 2006). These findings, which pretty much tally with many others, show that the British, while in some sense relatively at ease with 'immigrants', are also concerned about the possible disadvantages and dangers, and about the apparent collapse of the competence of their governmental systems: they want the security of knowing that immigration can be 'managed'. They could not have been reassured by the performance of Mr David Roberts, of the Immigration and Nationality Directorate of the Home Office, when he appeared in front of the House of Commons Home Affairs Committee:

> An MP: How many people are in Britain illegally?
> Mr Roberts: I haven't the faintest idea. An MP:
> How many failed asylum seekers are not removed?
> Mr Roberts: I haven't got that figure. An MP: How
> many people have been told to leave the country?
> Mr Roberts: I don't have that information.
> (*Daily Telegraph*, 17 May 2006)

It is very probable that the British people who responded to the surveys mentioned above had a conception of 'Justice, Equality and Fairness' that differs from that of the new Commission for Equality and Human Rights.

THE RACE RELATIONS (AMENDMENT) ACT 2000 AND THE EQUALITY ACT 2006

In the year 2000, the Race Relations Act of 1976 was amended to impose on over 43,000 public authorities a 'general duty' to 'eliminate unlawful discrimination and to promote equality of opportunity and good relations between persons of different racial groups'. The Commission for Racial Equality (CRE) commented that 'the aim of the duty is to make promotion of racial equality central to the work of the listed public authorities'. The legislation provided for regular audits of progress: the CRE web page gives examples of the triennial audits and documents on which should be recorded the response of each public authority. The CRE states that the legislation 'was necessary to ensure that we all receive the best from our public services. Previously, many public bodies were failing to address the problems of racial discrimination and inequality; this was highlighted by the inquiry into the murder of Stephen Lawrence.'

The Equality Act 2006 created a new Commission for Equality and Human Rights (CEHR), which brought together the work of the CRE, the Disability Rights Commission and the Equal Opportunities Commission. In addition, the CEHR will have responsibility for new laws on age, religion or belief, and sexual orientation, as well as for 'human rights'.

Police authorities and police forces are bound by the general duty and its auditing arrangements, as are all ministers and central government departments, schools, colleges and universities, professional bodies, etc. – a majority, that is, of the 6 million people who work in the public sector. This legislation represents a major success for multiculturalism. Amongst other things, the CEHR will

> promote and celebrate a diverse Britain, where there
> are good relations between groups, and people are
> not discriminated against because of their race,
> gender, disability, religion or belief, age or sexual
> orientation.
>
> (Equality Act, CEHR summary)

The Long March through the Commanding Heights (and Middle Depths) of British institutions is well under way, apparently unstoppable.

BOMB CULTURE

However, in the same decade as the new Act came the murders in New York and the murders on tube trains and a bus in London. A new and ferocious multiculturalism had arrived. It was associated with Islam, from which faith the killers came and in whose name (legitimately invoked or not, I do not know) they killed and died. The EU, as sensitive as ever to religious susceptibilities, produced a 'linguistic code of conduct', in which the term 'Islamic terrorism' was to be anathematised, to be replaced with 'terrorists who abusively invoke Islam'. The public were not quite so subtle; and while the Muslim Council of Britain's refrain of a pandemic of post-bomb 'Islamophobia' was both exaggerated and disingenuous, it was undoubtedly the case that in Britain, as in Holland, Belgium, France, Spain, Denmark – indeed in most of Europe – multiculturalism had, in the words of a pre-conference publicity sheet, 'taken a beating' (IMISCOE, conference on 'Reassessing Multiculturalism in Europe', University of Oxford, June/July 2006).

Many post-bomb multicultural gatherings and conferences were organised to deal with this new situation – or else found themselves, already gathered in seminar or conference, having to face up to an unexpected and terrifying item on the agenda. No multicultural expert had addressed (and no multicultural theory had been able or had seen fit to predict) the murderous actions of British-born Muslims, who came from reasonably comfortable backgrounds. For many multiculturalists, the response took on the nature of defiant calls to arms, multicultural rescue squads and hastily constructed laagers. Yet they and their colleagues were faced with bad news, when no less a personage than Trevor Phillips, the chairman of the CRE, called for the 'end of multiculturalism', referring to a society 'becoming more divided by race and religion', an '"anything goes" multiculturalism...which leads to deeper division and inequality'. German Chancellor Angela Merkel said that 'multiculturalism cannot succeed' and Gilles Keppel said that the bombers 'were the children of Britain's own multicultural society' (see Modood, 2005). It took a sociologist to come up with the right phrase for the right occasion: the Italian Giovanni Sartori decried 'an excess of *alterity*' (my translation).

AN EXCESS OF *ALTERITY*

Coupled with this perturbation in the multicultural camp has been the revelation of the demonstrable incompatibility of 'human rights' legislation with the exigent nature of life in the contemporary nation state, and the associated failure of our governmental systems to cope with the concomitant administrative and legal confusion. The criminal justice system, said Mr Blair, 'is the public service most distant from what reasonable people want' (*Daily Telegraph*, 16 May 2006).

The prime minister, belatedly, seems to have realised that it is hugely corrosive of the formal loyalties of an already battered citizenry to have to watch their public institutions crumble into incompetence under the pressure of a large, growing, and rather alien congeries of people to whom such 'law' as might (in theory) apply is deduced from legal principles that they, the general citizenry, neither understand nor support. What, reading the CEHR advertisement quoted at the start of this chapter, and then looking at the world around him, does the average citizen make of 'Justice, Equality, Fairness' in his or her society, which is already, and quite autochthonously, difficult to govern? As the Parekh Commission rightly understands, 'How a state sees and controls the borders between itself and others is of paramount importance' (Parekh, 2002: xiii). The British are watching the dissolution of their state.

On the one hand, we have tens of thousands of illegal immigrants and many hundreds of 'illegal' criminals, free from any effective control by the Home Office, the legal system or the prison service. The Home Office estimates that there are between 155,000 and 284,000 failed asylum seekers awaiting removal, but it does not know where most of them live.

Neither does it, or the Immigration Service, know how many hundreds of thousands more are coming in. Every year, hundreds of dangerous foreign criminals just walk out of Her Majesty's prisons, where 10,000 foreign prisoners now find themselves at any one time. Of London's 180 crime gangs, which together speak 24 languages, nearly half are 'ethnically based', making them almost opaque to the police (*The Times*, 26 April 2006). In July 2005, Robert Beckley, speaking as the representative of the Association of Chief Police Officers, told a large post-bomb gathering at the Regent's Park Mosque that 'the police service did not know much about the Muslim community, they policed "around", but not "in" it'. On top of that, of course, the police are, if not paralysed, then certainly slowed down by the demands of political correctness. What on earth are the Metropolitan Police to make of charges of 'racism' levelled at their *automatic number-plate recognition cameras* (*Sunday Times*, 14 May 2006)?

The Home Office is a mess: for the first time, in 2004/5, the National Audit Office refused to 'sign off' the Department's books because it could not match bank statements and receipts. To be fair, and to make reassurance doubly difficult, the Home Office is not alone.

MI5 is, it seems, unable to keep tabs on the 1,400–1,600 suspected al-Qaeda sympathisers at large in Britain, a 'guesstimate' already double that made by the same organisation a year before. Europe's 20 million refugees are 'managed' under a 60-year-old Convention designed to cope with a temporary problem after World War Two. This system evidently cannot cope now. The Child Support Agency overpays a billion pounds and can recover but a fraction of it. The National Health Service has just about doubled its income, and yet seems unable to manage, having spent (or wasted) £15 billion pounds on complex computer systems, and having contrived to pay GPs so much that they can now afford to retire early!

To be absolutely clear, the collapse of the state is only partly tied, causally or otherwise, to 'multiculturalism'. There is, to paraphrase the prime minister, simply too much illegality and too much incompetence about.

At the same time, and coming almost from another planet, we have the Equality Act and its associated legislative and administrative upheaval, all of which will have the effect of pushing the public sector towards becoming an anxious self-watching resource-consuming bloat, whose main product will be itself. This legislation destroys the distinction Max Weber made between the 'formal rationality' of a modern state, in which general laws apply equally to all citizens of the state, including its employees, and the administrative procedures of 'substantive rationality', in which 'a patrimonial prince bestows utilitarian and social ethical blessings upon his subjects, in the manner of the master of a large house upon the members of his household' (Weber, 1970: 298). As I suggested in Chapter 7, the Indian system of 'reservation' for backward and very backward classes gets close to Max Weber's prescription for the patrimonial prince. In India, there are probably justifications for such a system: it is a useful form of corruption, functioning primarily as a way of avoiding serious social unrest, which is a major compensation for the inevitable result – the notoriously slow, nepotistic style of life in Indian public services. In the USA and Canada, where such reservations or 'quotas' have been tried, and where society is not caste bound, they have not worked, and have done considerably more harm than good (Scull, 2006; Loney, 1998). While there soon may be a queue of people wishing to join the 'creamy layers' of the CEHR-policed public services, there will surely be substantial migration from them, too – either a physical departure by people, or else a migration of the mind, a withdrawal of commitment, a resort to cynicism, a general lowering of morale – not least on the part of the putative 'beneficiaries'. Canada, not India, is our likely fate:

> The dominance of the issue of identity politics, like the social and economic pressures resulting from high immigration levels, has the effect of crowding other issues off the stage. . . Canadians have financed an increasingly destructive agenda, whose outcome is not unity, equality or fairness, but division.
>
> (Loney, 1998: 332)

As and when the triennial review teams arrive in some portion of the public sector, and the reviews envisaged by the Equality Act and the Race Relations (Amendment) Act get into full swing, with the 'quota-results' and 'quota-caper' open to view and comment in the media, we will no doubt see an extension into public sector employment policies of the media style described by John Lloyd:

> The public sphere has not been seen as one to preserve, but as an area on which tournaments may be staged on the one hand, and on the other as a landscape dotted with forests, in whose depths reporters can hunt for prey, dragging them out into the light of day on the end of their spears.
>
> (Lloyd, 2004: 11)

Into such a world is the new Commission launched. The abolition of this Commission would be the single most useful act of political responsibility.

MEA CULPA, BUT NOT YET

> It is widely said by its critics that 'multiculturalism' is a vague, confused concept whose different meanings to different people render sensible debate and policy orientation difficult. There is some truth in this, but the same is true of its rival ideas or models, 'assimilation' and 'integration'.
>
> (Modood, 2005: 2)

In 2002, the Parekh Commission stated that 'Citizens are not only individuals but are also members of particular religious, ethnic, cultural and regional communities' (Parekh, 2002: ix). In 2001, Tariq Modood, adviser to the Parekh Commission, in a response to the attacks on the World Trade Center, insisted that 'We have to be careful not to cast our friends nor enemies in ethnic, religious or religious terms' (Modood, 2001: 1).

In such seemingly minor confusions – as well as in larger ways spelt out above – lies the evidence that multiculturalism is losing whatever coherence it once had. There are three major interlinked stratagems involved in 'rethinking multiculturalism', to borrow the title of Lord Parekh's 2002 book. I must stress that, to date, this rethinking leaves intact and without apology the basic themes of 'hard' or 'primitive' multiculturalism with which I have been concerned. There is nothing vague or confused about the fundamentals of the multicultural writings of the last 30 years or so. They involve, as I have argued: the denial and vilification of our indigenous culture; the resort to a specious quiverful of 'injustice-proving' statistics; the parade of dubious pedigrees; and the demands for privilege, masquerading as justice. These are all fully and unapologetically in place, casting a long shadow. It remains to be seen how genuinely the 'new' multiculturalists can modify or jettison this dubious inheritance.

THE STRATAGEMS

1. A famous victory

Here we learn that multiculturalism was a thing of and for its own time, and virtuous then, but that time has now passed, mission accomplished. There is something of a disinclination in this school of thought to face up to life in a society in which the children that were so lovingly brought into the world are now, as such children tend to be, indifferent to both instruction and correction. Nevertheless, a leading multiculturalist, Yasmin Alibhai-Brown, told the 2005 Centre for Research on Nationalism, Ethnicity and Multiculturalism (CRONEM) conference on 'The Future of Multicultural Britain' that multiculturalism had come into existence as a response to Margaret Thatcher. Mrs Thatcher had, said Ms Alibhai-Brown, sold everything, promoting 'high capitalism' and, in the process, creating a new 'Englishness'. As a response, an unspecified 'we' 'invented' multiculturalism; but now it doesn't exist and there is no need for it: it only serves the state, leading to 'vestiges of gratitude'. We should, she felt, now think of ourselves as South Africa after apartheid. Another speaker felt that there was not much of an opening in 'Englishness', but that 'Britishness' left 'more room for manoeuvre'. He seemed to think that 'empires' could be tolerant and pluralistic. He adduced Bernard Porter's recent book on the British Empire as suggesting that it was of major cultural concern to only a minority of the British people, the majority being thereby relatively immune to imperialistic attitudes. Indeed, the speaker felt that empires such as those of Austria-Hungary, Russia, the Ottomans – and even the Romans! – were more tolerant than generally thought. It was no longer necessary to be white to be British; 'British' has been de-emphasised, and so will 'English'; 'English' is no longer – will be no longer – an ethnic group, and the same goes for all European countries. Modern democracies are more like a conversation, it being a matter of choice as to whether to be integrated or fragmented.

Not quite on song, a younger contributor stated that 'trust is essential to democratic states'. For such societies to function, people should comply voluntarily with democratic decisions, trusting in legislators and the mechanisms for controlling them. In multicultures, though, people might well not understand each other; newcomers might not be willing to adapt to the host community. Yet, at the start of her talk, she insisted that what she had to say should *not* be construed as being against ethnic diversity, *as such*, or *per se,* but against ethnic diversity *policies, as such* and *per se.* She later told me that she *had* to say that, otherwise she might have incurred the dread charge of promoting the idea of a dominant culture, the much-dreaded *hegemony.*

A victory of sorts, then: multiculturalism, a good idea in its time, can now be put to one side. We still await a formal repudiation of the Equality Act and the CEHR.

2. A New World

In this second stratagem, the starting point is that the world into which multiculturalism came has indeed changed, *and* that the children referred to above are the pioneers and exemplary citizens of this new, better world. In this world, the victories of the past are to be the basis of the programme for the future. Of central importance, and convenience, here is the idea of 'Europe'. As a geopolitical construct, 'Europe' provides the opportunity to continue to deny the reality of 'nation', with its concomitant pressure to have to choose to become a 'citizen' of one country as opposed to another. The problems of loyalty are solved, therefore, by being avoided. 'Europe' is both an alias and an alibi. Whereas nations do exist, 'Europe' doesn't; even in its non-existence it supersedes nations, which anyway shouldn't exist. In Europe, furthermore, 'human rights', in the absence of nation states, make some sense: as Lord Falconer told the Hansard Society, 'subscription to those rights is the entry price to a wider Europe' (Falconer, 2006: 3). Coupled with a consistent anti-Americanism, 'Europe' thus provides a loose covering for a retained and reinvigorated ethnic or religious multiculturalism. No, then, to nation state. Yes, then, to 'Europe'.

Europe is an attractive option for, among others, Muslims. I have, in the chapter on Islam, referred to the ideas of Dr Tariq Ramadan, an exponent of 'Islam in Europe'. Other writers, too, see the advantage of a 'Europeanised' multiculturalism – certainly for Muslims. Nezar AlSayyad and Manuel Castells are sure that 'Europe is once again becoming a land of Islam' (note the 'once again'). The EU and NATO are taking over the key functions of the (old) states. The old states are breaking down into regional and sub-regional ethnicities: there is 'an increasing decoupling between the instrumentality of the state (i.e. citizenship) and the ethnic, cultural and roots of identity'. Demography is on the side of ethnic minorities, as 'Germany, like other European countries, is set to completely change its demographic structure within the next twenty years'. Europe is set to become a 'borderland', 'an interstitial zone of displacement and deterritorialization that shapes the identity of the hybridized subject'. These borderlands are not 'fragments of the in-between [because] the most hybrid of places have moved firmly to the center of the core'. The only problem 'with Europe today is not that it is not multiethnic but that it does not consider itself multiethnic' (AlSayyad and Castells, 2002: 1–3, 28).

This view of what Europe is – not 'European', not made of substantial nation states – is coupled with a hostile attitude to America. Again, Muslim writers make the strongest case. Modood insists that 'Muslim populations suffer depredations, occupation, ethnic cleansing and massacres with little action by the civilized world or the international community. Indeed, the latter, especially American power and military hardware, is often the source of the destruction and terror' (Modood, 2001: 2). Furthermore, 'British involvement with the United States's [sic] geopolitical projects – including the creation of Saudi-backed jihadism in Afghanistan in the 1980s as well as those following 9/11 – is certainly part of the current crisis and is putting great strain on multiculturalism' (Modood, 2005: 7). The new 'centre-left' coalition to which Modood aspires is anti-American, practically synonymous with being 'anti-war'.

As such, this 'new' multiculturalism is very specific to post-Cold War Europe, a continent weary of a century of conflict and war, sceptical of values such as nationalism or patriotism, indifferent to religion, welcoming relativism, immured in unearned affluence and self-aggrandisement, practising a lazy form of democracy, hazily committed to international agencies such as the UN, ashamed of its own history as warmaker and imperialist, uncomfortable in the shadow of its great protector, Christian America – a Europe, in fact, to which the multicultural meta-narrative is fish, fowl and fair red herring. In this image of the world, 'Europe' becomes something wholly different both from its own past and from the rip-roaring unregenerate conflict-full global present. Around it will swirl the rivalries of the 'quasi-imperial supernations' (CRONEM, 2005), but Old Europe can be seen, with the societies of Eastern Europe, as engaged in a unique process of stripping out the moral and political predicates of national life, replacing narrow war-competent nationalisms with an amiable, tolerant, boundary-indifferent pacifism. Such a society can be seen as a form of conversation, no longer grounded in notions of the social contract, or in Aristotle's idea of the necessity of a single idea of 'The Good', such singleness now made redundant (*ibid.*). In Europe, this tiny bit of the world, surrounded by the 'quasi-imperial super-nations' and assailed by the Dispossessed and the Enragés of the world, a polite 'conversation' will take place, concerned with little but its own civility and the avoidance of offence.

This is an extraordinary vision, but one well in keeping with the blind and zealous utopianism of the multicultural Project Mark II, and quite in keeping with its old antipathy to each separate nation state. Meanwhile, in the rest of the world, not so signally blessed with unproblematic guaranteed peace, the quasi-imperial super-nations like India and China (which together comprise about 40 per cent of the world's population) are confident, economically successful, self-assertive, well-armed nation states, mobilising and insistent on an overall national loyalty as the basis of their prosperity and strength, and determined to throw their weight around. Even in Africa, an appalling mess if ever there was one, what possibility there is of progress is seen to lie precisely in systems and structures of nationhood – structures to the creation of which their more responsible leaders dedicate themselves. In 'the West', America – the heir and exemplar of our culture at its most vigorous (warts and all) – finds itself at odds with European decadence. And yet, all the while, it has been American military dogged-ness that has made Europe and European decadence possible. It is, astoundingly enough, the American connection that our multiculturalists see as the main obstacle to their new project. Even so, Europe must be different.

To paraphrase Dorothy Parker, this is not a scenario to be tossed aside lightly: it should be thrown with great force.

3. Not enough, try harder, demand more

The third stratagem insists that if multiculturalism to date has not worked, then that is because it has not been given a full and proper outing. It has not been fully articulated, nor has its force been fully experienced. Tariq Modood, aware that there is a 'rising chorus of belief to the contrary', insists that 'multicul-turalism is still an attractive and worthwhile project; and that indeed we need more of it rather than less' (Modood, 2005: 2).

To some commentators, this suggestion of 'more' is simply because ethnic minorities resident in Britain are a fact, and that is that. For others, bombs, riots and other ructions have revealed a hitherto rather obscured truth about ethnic minorities: that some of them, at least, are more defined by their religion than by the colour of their skin or their place of birth. Again, of course, the reference is to Islam. Thus, wrote Professor Modood in 2002, the Rushdie affair 'mobilized an impassioned activism that no previous campaign against racism had been remotely able to stir' (Modood, 2002: 119). Muslims 'discovered a new community solidarity. . .what was striking was that even when the public rage against Muslims was at its most intense, Muslims neither sought nor were offered any special solidarity by any nonwhite minority' (*ibid*.: 119). Mr Rushdie has himself 'come to adopt a more pluralistic perspective, and one in which the Muslim presence is seen as a fact to be ignored at one's peril' (*ibid*.: 114).

The new multiculturalism must take on board the issues of *religious* discrimination and the demand for parity with native religions. Unusually, the secular–liberal Establishment, normally keen multiculturalists, turned out to be deeply unhappy with Muslim consciousness in the 1990s, thus breaking the old 'rainbow coalition'. The 'rise of Muslim assertiveness' has caused 'panic' and 'knee-jerk inconsistencies' among secular multiculturalists, and 'the result is a mixed up situation': 'In Britain multiculturalism continues to make political headway, while, paradoxically, the opposition between rival versions of multiculturalism deepens' (*ibid*.: 126–7). In another, somewhat camouflaged, revision of multiculturalism, we find a recognition that 'some versions of Islamism are not sufficiently respectful of fellow British citizens and the aspirations of a plural Britain' (Modood, 2005). Still 'very few minority people see egg-breaking and endless games of hardball as what the situation needs' (email from Modood, 7 October 2005, to CRONEM web discussion). We 'need to go further with multiculturalism, but it has to be a multiculturalism that is allied to, indeed is the other side of the coin of, a renewed and reinvigorated Britishness' (Modood, 2005: 7).

THE END OF LIBERALISM?

Modood is not alone in seeing, now, some advantage in 'Britishness': Parekh, Alibhai-Brown and Trevor Phillips all join in. It is, though, difficult to see how this 'new' multiculturalism can live contentedly with 'Britishness', given the attitudes, implicit and explicit, both in the great mound of earlier multicultural writings and in the less than positive ways in which they now seek to approach their new task. Did Mr Rushdie, for example, spontaneously really 'come to adopt a more pluralistic perspective', or was he more impressed with the evident peril of ignoring his co-religionists? Most worryingly, Modood now wants to challenge and debate not just the 'hegemony' of our national culture, but the very systems of liberty under which our national debates have been conducted for so long. He wishes to repudiate 'the classical liberal identification of the political with the realms of law and the state' (Modood, 2002: 117). He disputes the distinction liberalism makes between the private and the public space; and he disputes the very idea of a 'discursive space', in which political debate takes place and disputes are resolved. This theory, he says, acts *inter alia* as a '"gag-rule" to exclude matters of concern to marginalized and subordinated groups'. 'Laws and policies may be of lesser importance than the very process of dialogue' (*ibid.*).

Since that was published, we have had a debate on a law about 'incitement to religious hatred', and we have had murder bombing on the London Underground and deaths caused by the violence of Muslim reaction to the publication of some cartoons in Denmark. These, and other, events have exacerbated the tensions in the liberal-secular multicultural consensus, there being nothing particularly liberal or particularly secular in making a point by killing people in the name of religion. Islam stands wrapped in the uncomfortable coat of 'exceptionalism', being both illiberal and anti-secular. Liberal secularists, generally both anti-religion and anti-special treatment, were clearly at risk of abandoning the multicultural enterprise when it seemed to be becoming mobilised in support of one, somewhat intolerant, religion. They would, however, be perhaps more likely to remain steadfast in a continuing and revitalised anti-*racist* campaign. The rosorially multiloquous Modood sought to save the liberal-secular day by advocating the reclassification of Islam as a *race* rather than a religion. In this way, Islamic 'exceptionalism' would be camouflaged:

> Once we break with the idea that (contemporary) racism is only about biology or that racism is of one classical kind, then the idea of a pure racism should lose its social science appeal. We should be able to see that cultural groups and religious groups can be racialised: that Muslims can be the victims of racism *qua* Muslim as well as *qua* Asians or Arabs or Bosnians. . . For me it is possible to imagine a (not necessarily likely) Britain of the future where the only non-whites that suffer racism are Muslims.
>
> (Modood, 2006: 57)

Modood is a leading and rather typical example of the multicultural establishment. He is an academic, holding a chair at Bristol University, where he heads the Centre for the Study of Ethnicity and Citizenship. He is an habitué of the 'quango' world, at the CRE and the London Policy Studies Institute. He is an adviser to the Muslim Council of Britain, a practising Muslim one assumes. He personifies, therefore – and in his vocabulary he expresses – the very real and very dangerous mess into which British multiculturalism has taken us. What, for example, are we to make of the following?

> In relation to free speech my strategy has been, firstly, to assimilate Muslims into existing legal provisions by extending the widely supported need in contemporary democracies for an offence of incitement to racial hatred to incitement to religious hatred and group defamation. Secondly, to protect the Millian value of unfettered pursuit of truth by defining it more narrowly as free inquiry rather than as free expression.
>
> (Modood, 2006: 52)

The 'Millian' reference is, of course, to that very British philosopher, John Stuart Mill. We are entitled to wonder, I think, what Mill would make of an academic drawing a distinction between 'free inquiry' and 'free expression'. This seems to me to be far removed from the liberal Britishness to which our multiculturalists now, apparently, aspire. It is, perhaps, a measure of the 'mixed up situation' that we are in that Professor Modood's New Multiculturalism seems more of a threat than a promise – to all of us. I hope I misunderstand him.

CONCLUSION

Bombs are clearly a problem. So are riots. Muslims have broken the multicultural consensus. It is difficult to count as fellow strugglers in the same cause such erstwhile and errant brethren. Yasmin Alibhai-Brown tells the story of a woman in a face-covering *niqab* who came to see her, having followed her home. She had been beaten up by her family, her father and brothers. In a way, the details are too dreadful to recount and do not, perhaps, matter. Ms Alibhai-Brown points to the 'thousands of liberal Muslims who would dearly like the state to take a stand on their behalf. If it doesn't, it will betray vulnerable British citizens and the nation's most cherished principles and encourage Islam to move back even faster into the dark ages, when we all need to face the future together' (*The Week*, 7 January 2006). It is good to hear, from the mouth of such as Ms Alibhai-Brown, of the existence of such things as 'the nation's most cherished principles' and of their ability to prevent Islam from moving back to the dark ages – or, if I understand Ms Alibhai-Brown's syntax correctly, to at least slow it down as it heads in that direction.

Muslims are not the only ones to take a strong multicultural stand. Sikhs have rioted in Birmingham, forcing the closure of a play, injuring policemen, and sending the author into hiding. The police made arrests, but no serious penalties have been visited upon the rioters. The theatre closed because Sikh representatives, in the presence of the police, said that they could not (would not?) guarantee that there would be no more violence. Amardeep Bassey, a Sikh journalist on the Birmingham *Sunday Mercury*, analyses this event as proof of an internecine battle for power between rival Sikh groups: 'an internal battle for influence. . .and an external battle for the same level of recognition as British Muslims' (*The Birmingham Rep Riot: Behind the Scenes*, BBC Radio 4, 23 August 2005).

British Hindus are seldom in the news in such a way, but it would be a mistake to think that the Sangh Parivar and its ideology of *Hindutva* are for domestic, Indian, consumption only. Only recently, Hindu threats of violence forced the closure of an exhibition of the paintings of M. F. Husain at Asia House, in London (*Observer*, 18 May 2006). Once again, the police do nothing. Europe might be a war-weary, cynical place; but most ethnic minority religions have a strong stiffening of True Believers within them. Supine politicians and affable 'community' police will do nothing but feed these beasts and get them wanting more – from us, and from each other.

Ironically, perhaps, it is to a leading official multiculturalist that we must turn for a comment on the 'new' multiculturalism. In 2005, Trevor Phillips reacted to these new aspects of multiculturalism by saying that Britain was 'sleepwalking to segregation'. In October 2005, the *Muslim Weekly* ('The Voice for Muslims in Britain') reported that Mr Phillips now felt that we need 'a highway code for the multi-ethnic society'. The 'Director of Equalities and Policing for the Mayor of London', Lee Jasper, said in response that the chairman of the Commission for Racial Equality (Mr Phillips) should 'seriously consider whether he is in the right job'. Mr Phillips' offence was to query the necessity for leaflets in multiple languages, and to wonder whether the term 'coloured' really was offensive, or whether Muslim pupils (always, of course, Muslim girls) should be allowed to vary or ignore school uniforms. Mr Phillips went too far for the *Muslim Weekly*. It quoted – in retaliation almost – a Runnymede Trust report that *inter alia* said that the British Empire was founded on the same principles as Nazi Germany. Mr Phillips, reported the *Muslim Weekly*, was chairman of the Runnymede Trust, thus declaring to the world that the 'word British was tainted with racism'. I assume that the reference was to the Parekh Report!

To the evident perturbation of the *Muslim Weekly*, Mr Phillips was now reported as regarding the British Empire as proof that 'the British people are not, by nature, bigots'. Phillips continued:

> It would be a travesty to suggest that a people who endured two devastating wars in the first half of the last century, in order to ward off tyranny, not just from these islands but from the whole of Europe, would be so small minded as to say that we could not live with the Polish airmen, the French resistance fighters, the Caribbean mechanics, and the Indian infantrymen who also played a heroic role in that struggle.
>
> (*Muslim Weekly*, 7 October 2005)

One might query Mr Phillips' list (French resistance fighters??), but he went further. At the Conservative Party's Blackpool conference, again as reported in the *Muslim Weekly*, he said: 'We are used to the idea of one nation. That is why the prospect of a Britain fragmented by race and religion is so alien to us. It is simply not in our nature' (*ibid.*). The *Muslim Weekly*'s attitude to Mr Phillips illustrates the problem faced by our would-be new multiculturalists: they trail a sticky past behind them.

Alain Finkielkraut quotes Hannah Arendt in *The Burden of Our Time*. She says that the predominant mood of modern man is 'resentment', a complex term in any translation. It seems to me to describe the tone of much multicultural writing, as if the world is full – and full only – of malice and envy, of failure and injustice, of everything being someone else's deliberate and malevolent fault. In Trevor Phillips' comments above, we see an example of someone getting close to what Arendt presents as the opposite, or counter, to 'resentment', i.e. 'gratitude':

> A fundamental gratitude for the few elementary things that indeed are invariably given us, such as life itself, the existence of man and the world. In the

> sphere of politics, gratitude emphasises that we are
> not alone in this world. We can reconcile ourselves
> to the variety of mankind, to the differences between
> human beings. . .only through insight into the
> tremendous bliss that man was created with the
> power of procreation, that not a single man but
> MEN inhabit the earth.
>
> (Finkielkraut, 2001: 112)

There is little sense of gratitude in British multicultural writing: gratitude for the country in which the multicultural-ists live, which, with all its faults, is freer, safer and more open to their talents than any of the countries from which most of them come. England is not more beautiful than Pakistan; nor is it as astounding as India or Africa. It is small, dingy, and tightly occupied. It has flat pavements, a reliable water sup-ply, sewers that work. It has an army that is either abroad, in civvies or in barracks: in many other territories of the world, the army is a form of domestic terror! Its police do not, as a rule, carry guns (and are evidently incompetent when they do have to use them).

We, the British, are indeed responsible for some nasty and exploitative acts. We are not, however – either alone or with our allies – responsible for all the mess in the world. And when the world calls for help, it calls on us, and on societies like ours.

There is nothing magic or God-given in our apparent sta-bility, in our flat pavements and functioning sewers. We have not solved the problem of social order (who has?), and this society, like any other, needs care and consideration – not the ignorant sneers of guests or the propagation of invitations to make war upon us, in word or in deed. No one has to live here.

We have a way of making collective decisions: this way is wrangle-edged and imperfect, but is better than a bullet or a riot. Some people are poorer than others, but they are not condemned to remain that way, and the truth of that is embodied in the family histories of me and many others. My grandparents were poorer than any Pakistani immigrant;

though you would have had a fight on your hands had you called them 'poor'. I do not speak the language of my grandfathers, who were thrashed in school if they spoke it, but why whinge about English hegemony? I resent having my 'bit' of Great Britain, whether Wales or, now, the North East, wheeled out as some surrogate ally in the multicultural game of unravelling the United Kingdom.

Do not break what you cannot mend. Mind your manners. Be grateful: you are a guest in my country. Welcome.

REFERENCES

Notes:

(1) Like many writers, I increasingly rely on the 'Web' for information. For novices like me, this can sometimes have the effect of complicating and even confusing the retrieval and presentation of data. In particular, the date of getting access to an article on a web site is not the same as the date of deposition of the article on that site. I apologise, to author and reader, in advance for the occasions when my inexperience and incompetence may lead to some vagueness.

(2) In the chapter on India, I rely to a large extent on the English-language Indian press, such as *The Vijay Times, The Hindu, The Deccan Herald,* etc. I realise that such newspapers are but a small part of the world of the Indian Press.

(3) Frequently consulted websites include:
www.firstworldwar.com – for primary documents on World War One.
www.hindustantimes.com – *Hindustan Times* newspaper online.

Al-Moghamis, N., 2002, *Christianity and Islam According to the Bible and the Qur'an,* Darussalam Publishers, Riyadh, Saudi Arabia.

AlSayyad, N., and Castells, M., 2002, *Muslim Europe or Euro-Islam: Politics, Culture and Civilization in the Age of Globalization,* Lexington Books.

Ameli, S. R. (ed.), 2004, *British Muslims' Expectation of Government*, Islamic Human Rights Commission.

Anderson, D., 2004, *All Oiks Now: The Unnoticed Surrender of Middle England*, Social Affairs Unit.

As-Saheem, M. A., 1999, *Christianity: The Original and the Present Reality*, Darussalam Publishers, Riyadh, Saudi Arabia.

Athale, Anil, 2006, 'Muslims in the army: A dangerous census', 14 February, at http://in.rediff.com/news/2006/feb/14guest.htm

Ballard, R., 1987, 'The political economy of migration: Pakistan, Britain and the Middle East', in J. Eades, *Migrants, Workers and the Social Order*, Tavistock.

Book of Common Prayer, 1662, Eyre and Spottiswoode.

Brown, Gordon, 2006, 'A modern view of Britishness', a speech to the Fabian Society, 14 January.

Center for Religious Freedom, 2003, *The Rise of Hindu Extremism and the Repression of Christian and Muslim Minorities in India*, Freedom House.

Chandler, D., 1994, *Oxford Illustrated History of the British Army*, Oxford University Press.

CRONEM (Centre for Research on Nationalism, Ethnicity and Multiculturalism), 2005, Conference on the Future of Multicultural Britain, 14–15 June, own notes.

Davies, J. G., 1985, *Asian Housing in Britain*, Social Affairs Unit.

—— 1995, *The Christian Warrior in the Twentieth Century*, Edwin Mellen Press.

Defoe, D., 1936, 'The English race', in D. N. Smith (ed.), *Oxford Book of Eighteenth-Century Verse*, Oxford University Press.

'Demographics of the armed forces', 2006, posting on South Asian website, 19 February, at www.thesouthasian.org/archives/2006/demographics_of_the_armed_forc.html

Dennis, N., and Erdos, G., 2005, *Cultures and Crimes: Policing in Four Nations*, Civitas.

Dennis, N., Erdos, G., and Al-Shahi, A., 2000, *Racist Murder and Pressure Group Politics: The Macpherson Report and the Police*, Civitas.

Enan, M. Abdullah, 2001, *Decisive Moments in the History of Islam*, Goodword Books, New Delhi.

Falconer, Lord, 2006, 'Democratic renewal: Reform of Parliament and public life', speech to the Hansard Society, 16 May, at www.dca.gov.uk/speeches/2006/sp060516.htm

Finkielkraut, A., 2000, *In the Name of Humanity, Reflections on the Twentieth Century*, Pimlico.

Fraser, D., 2006, *A Land Fit for Criminals: An Insider's View of Crime, Punishment, and Justice in the UK*, Book Guild.

Friedman, T., 2006, *The World is Flat*, Penguin.

Gellner, E., 1994, *Conditions of Liberty: Civil Society and its Rivals*, Hamish Hamilton.

Glees, A., and Pope, C., 2005, *When Students turn to Terror: Terrorism and Extremist Activity on British Campuses*, Social Affairs Unit.

Green, S. J. D., and Whiting, R. C., 2002, *The Boundaries of the State in Modern Britain*, Cambridge University Press.

Grewal, J. S., 1990, *The Sikhs of the Punjab*, New Cambridge History of India, Cambridge University Press.

Hadow, W. H., 1923, *Citizenship*, Oxford University Press.

Hamdi, W. M. S., 1987, *Rashid Ali al-Gailani: The Nationalist Movement in Iraq, 1939–41*, Darf Publishers, London.

Hardy, P., 1972, *The Muslims of British India*, Cambridge University Press.

Himmelfarb, G., 1995, *The De-moralization of Society: From Victorian Virtues to Modern Values*, Institute of Economic Affairs, Health and Welfare Unit.

Hinnells, J., 2000, 'South Asian religions in migration', in *The South Asian Religious Diaspora in Britain, Canada and the United States*, State University of New York Press.

Hochschild, A., 2005, *Bury the Chains: The British Struggle to Abolish Slavery*, Macmillan.

Holt, R., 1992, *Sport and the British*, Oxford University Press.

Home Office, *Public Service Agreement – Community Safety and Justice 2008/9 to 2010/11*, at http://lcjb.cjsonline. gov.uk/ncjb/library/psa_consultation.pdf

Howard, Anthony, 2005, *Basil Hume, the Monk Cardinal*, Hodder Headline.

Humaid, Sheikh A. bin M. bin, 1995, *Jihad in the Qur'an and the Sunnah*, Darussalam Publishers, Riyadh.

Huntington, S., 2002, *The Clash of Civilizations and the Remaking of World Order*, Free Press.

IMISCOE (International Migration, Integration and Social Cohesion), 2006, 'Reassessing multiculturalism in Europe', Conference at Oxford, June/July.

Institute for the Study of Islam and Christianity, 2005, *Islam in Britain*, Isaac Publishing.

Ipgrave, M. (ed.), 2004, *Scriptures in Dialogue: Christians and Muslims Studying the Bible and the Qur'an together*, Church House Publishing.

Jameelah, M., 1977, *Islam versus the West*, Mohammad Yusuf Khan, Lahore.

Khalistan Affairs Center, 2006, 'The Indian Army refuses to provide data to the Sachar Committee on the number of Muslims in its ranks', 22 February, at www.khalistan-affairs.org/home/khalistancalling/2006/february22.aspx

Khan, Syed Ahmed, 1998, 'One country, two nations', in H. D. Sharma (ed.), *100 Best Pre-Independence Speeches 1870–1947*, HarperCollins, New Delhi, pp.19–22.

Krishnan, P. S., 2006, 'The socio-historical and constitutional perspective and imperatives of the proposed bill', *Frontline – India's National Magazine*, vol. 23, issue 8, April/May.

Kureisha, H., 1990, *The Buddha of Suburbia*, Faber and Faber.

Larkin, P., 2003, 'Church going', in *Collected Poems*, Faber and Faber.

Lassner, P., 2004, *Colonial Strangers: Women Writing the End of the British Empire*, Rutgers University Press.

Levy, A., 1999, *Fruit of the Lemon*, quoted in M. Stein, 2004, *Black British Literature: Novels of Transition*, Ohio State University Press, p. 72.

Lewis, B., 1970, *The Arabs in History*, Hutchinson.

Lloyd, J., 2004, *What the Media are Doing to our Politics*, Constable.

Loney, M., 1998, *The Pursuit of Division: Race, Gender, and Professional Hiring in Canada*, McGill-Queen's University Press.

Malik, A. A. (ed.), 2006, *The State We Are In: Identity, Terror and the Law of Jihad*, Amal Press.

McLagan, G., 2005, *Guns and Gangs: Inside Black Gun Crime*, Allison and Busby Limited.

Meredith, M., 2006, *The State of Africa: A History of Fifty Years of Independence*, Free Press.

Modood, T., 1992, *Not Easy Being British: Colour, Culture and Citizenship*, Runnymede Trust and Trentham Books.

—— (ed.), 1997, *Church, State and Religious Minorities*, Policy Studies Institute.

—— 2001, *Muslims in the West: A Positive Asset*, SSRC (accessed April 2006), at www.ssrc.org/ sept11/essays/modood.htm

—— 2002, 'The place of Muslims in British secular multi-culturalism', in N. AlSayyad and M. Castells (eds), *Muslim Europe or Euro-Islam: Politics, Culture and Citizenship in the Age of Globalization*, Lexington Books.

—— 2005, 'Remaking multiculturalism after 7/7', Open Democracy website, 29 September 2005, at www.open-democracy.net/conflict-terrorism/ multiculturalism_2879.jsp

Modood, T. *et al.*, 2006, 'The Danish cartoon affair: Free speech, racism, Islamism, and integration,' *International Migration*, vol. 44 (5), pp. 3–57.

Mohanty, J., 2004, 'Azad Hind Fauj and Provisional government: A saga of Netaji', *Orissa Review*, August, at www.orissa.gov.in/e-magazine/Orissareview/ aug2004/engishPdf/Pages1–3.pdf

Morris, H., 1989, *We Will Remember Them: A Record of the Jews who Died in the Armed Forces of the Crown 1939–1945*, Brassey's, Pergamon.

Muslim Council of Britain, 2005, *Electing to Deliver.*

Narendran, K. K., 2004, *Report of Shri Justice Narendran's Commission*, Centre for Legal Education and Development Studies, Thiruvananthapuram, Kerala, India.

Olsover, L., 1980, *The Jewish Communities of North East England*, Ashley Mark Publishing.

Orwell, G., 1957, *Inside the Whale and Other Essays*, Penguin Books.

Owusu, K. (ed.), *Black British Culture and Society: A Text Reader*, Routledge.

Parekh, B., 2002, *The Future of Multi-Ethnic Britain*, Report of the Commission on the Future of Multi-Ethnic Britain, Profile Books.

Pattie, C. *et al.*, 2004, *Citizenship in Britain: Values, Participation and Democracy*, Cambridge University Press.

Phillips, M., and Phillips, T., 1999, *WINDRUSH: The Irresistible Rise of Multi-Racial Britain*, HarperCollins.

Pieterse, J. N., and Parekh, B., 1995, *The Decolonization of Imagination: Culture, Knowledge and Power*, Zed Books.

Platt, L., 2005, *Migration and Social Mobility: The Life Chances of Britain's Minority Ethnic Communities*, Polity Press.

Porter, B., 2004, *The Absent-Minded Imperialists: Empire, Society and Culture in Britain*, Oxford University Press.

Ramadan, T., 2001, *Islam, the West and the Challenges of Modernity*, trans. Said Amghar, The Islamic Foundation.

—— 2006, 'An Islamic reformation', *Dispatches*, Channel 4, 1 May.

Ramu, P. S., 1998, *Azad Hind Fauj and the Freedom Movement*, Vedams Books, New Delhi.

Sarila, N. S., 2005, *The Shadow of the Great Game: The Untold Story of Indian Partition*, HarperCollins, India.

Scull, A., 2006, 'Class action', *TLS*, 7 April, a review article of W. G. Bowen *et al.*, 2004, *Equity and Excellence in American Higher Education*, University of Virginia Press, and D. Bok, 2004, *Our Underachieving Colleges*, Princeton University Press.

Shari'ati, A., 1986, *What is to be Done: The Enlightened Thinkers and an Islamic Renaissance*, Institute for Research and Islamic Studies, Houston, Texas.

Siddiqui, K., 1983, *Issues in the Islamic Movement 1981–82 (1401–1402)*, Open Press Ltd., London.

Silberman, B. S., 1993, *Cages of Reason: The Rise of the Rational State in France, Japan, the United States and Great Britain*, University Press of Chicago.

Simon, J. L., 1997, *The State of Humanity*, Blackwell.

Smith, Z., 2000, *White Teeth*, Hamish Hamilton.

Sowell, T., 2000, *Basic Economics: A Citizen's Guide to the Economy*, Basic Books.

Stein, M., 2004, *Black British Literature: Novels of Transition*, Ohio State University Press.

Taylor, J., 1976, *The Half-way Generation: A Study of Asian Youths in Newcastle upon Tyne*, NFER Publishing Company Ltd.

Tejpal, T., 2006, 'Democracy; miracle train of myriad millions', *TEHELKA, the People's Paper*, 11 February, at www.tehelka.com/story_main16.asp?filename=In021106 Miracle_train_p03.asp

Thomson, A., and Ur'Rahim, M., 2004, *Islam in Andalus*, Ta-Ha Publishers.

Thomson, Mike, 2004, 'Hitler's secret Indian army', BBC News online, 23 September, at http://news.bbc.co.uk/1/hi/world/europe/3684288.stm

Thompson, A., 1940, *Enlist India for Freedom!*, Victory Books No. 5, London.

United Nations, 2003, *Trends in Total Migrant Stock*.

Weber, Max, 1970, *From Max Weber*, ed. Hans Gerth and C. Wright Mills, Routledge and Kegan Paul.

West, P., 2005, *The Poverty of Multiculturalism*, Civitas.

'Who was the Grand Mufti, Haj Muhammed Amin al-Husseini?', no date, at www.palestinefacts.org/pf_mandate_grand_mufti.php

Wills, G., 1992, *Lincoln at Gettysburg: The Words that Remade America*, Simon and Schuster.